Conviction
Vs
Mercy

Merging the Two

in Dealing with Modern Spiritual Challenges

Conviction Versus Mercy

Merging the Two in Dealing with

Modern Spiritual Challenges

Gardner Hall

Mount Bethel Publishing
Port Murray, New Jersey

Conviction Versus Mercy

Merging the Two to Deal with Modern Spiritual Challenges

All scripture references, unless otherwise specified, are taken from the NEW AMERICAN STANDARD BIBLE®, Copyright © 1960,1962,1963,1968,1971,1972,1973,1975,1977,1995 by The Lockman Foundation. Used by permission. Other versions quoted are the King James Version (KJV), the New King James Version (NKJV) and the English Standard Version (ESV)

Published by Mount Bethel Publishing,
P.O. Box 123, Port Murray, NJ 07865,
www.MountBethelPublishing.com

ISBN: 978-0-9850059-2-4
Library of Congress Control Number: 2013906333

Cover Design: Kirby Davis

Dedicated to my daughter, Leah, who wants to grow in

Christ more than anything else.

Contents

Interaction Between Conviction and Mercy through the Centuries

Beverly and I liked Sherry, a young woman who came to our apartment in Buenos Aires, Argentina in 1980 to talk to her family in the States on our ham (shortwave) radio. We knew that she believed in the goodness of God, but also knew that she held some significantly different views regarding Bible teaching than we did.

One day, one of those differences came up and we began to discuss it. I quoted a verse to her which I believed would open her eyes to the truth. I suppose I expected her to offer an objection to my interpretation of the Bible passage or suggest that we look at another scripture that in her mind would shed light on what we had just read. However, she just looked at me, smiled sweetly and said,

"If that's what you want that verse to say, it's fine with me. I just prefer to look at it a different way."

"How do you look at it?" I asked.

She smiled again and said, "I'll just keep that to myself. You see it your way and I'll see it mine. All that matters is love."

I didn't realize it at the time but as I look back I realize Sherry had introduced me to "Christian" Postmodernism.

There has been a revolution in dominant philosophical thought in the Western world that has replaced the three hundred year supremacy of Modernism/Rationalism with Postmodernism. The revolution, which has occurred in the last fifty years, has affected almost every aspect of human life: art, politics, education and religion. Its impact has reached into churches of every stripe. Those influenced primarily by religious rationalism, often over forty years of age, find themselves in conflict with those who are increasingly affected by Postmodernism, often under forty years of age. Meanwhile, the teachings of Jesus Christ, which should supersede philosophical trends in the minds of his followers, are often overlooked in the controversies.

Colossians 2:8-10

The apostle Paul was very graphic when warning against being overly influenced by worldly philosophies.

See to it that no one takes you captive through philosophy and empty deception, according to the tradition of men, according to the elementary principles of the world, rather than according to Christ.

For in Him all the fullness of Deity dwells in bodily form, and in Him you have been made complete, and He is the head over all rule and authority;

"Take captive" - This term is found only here in the New Testament[1] and refers to taking someone as booty in war. Human philosophies can wash our brains to the point that we become like helpless captives.

Michael (not his real name) was raised by Christians but took a number of classes in college such as sociology, feminism and various literature classes that emphasized modern philosophical concepts. He began to struggle spiritually. When speaking to him now about simple principles of the gospel of Christ I can sense that his mind is racing as he tries to filter what he is hearing through the humanist philosophies with which he's been indoctrinated. How I wish he could fully enjoy the peace and purpose that Christ gives, but he has been brainwashed, "taken captive," through empty worldly philosophies that are depriving him of the joy of Christ. I still pray that he can be rescued.

• **"Through philosophy"** - This term is also found only here in the New Testament and was a favorite of the Gnostics whom Paul may have been combating.[2]

• **According to the elementary principles of the world** - Most high sounding philosophies are designed to do little more than justify man in his desire to do whatever he wants in order to satisfy his flesh and stroke his pride.

• **We don't need worldly philosophies!** Man wasn't designed to be taken captive by them to live empty lives. Rather he has everything he needs in Jesus Christ.

Three Major Philosophical Epochs

Louis Hoffman, a postmodern proponent of "existential therapy" says there have been three major philosophical epochs in the Western World in the last five hundred years:[3]

(1) Premodernism (up to 1650) - Hoffman said, "In premodern times it was believed that Ultimate Truth could be known and the way to this knowledge is through direct revelation. This direct revelation was generally assumed to come from God or a god."

This doesn't sound harmful, but its flaw was that the church was assumed to be the source of this knowledge from God and its prejudices and politics greatly muddied the waters in its dispensing of "Ultimate Truth."

(2) Modernism (1650 - 1950s) - There are at least two major philosophical approaches (or, epistemologies) of Modernism: (a) knowing truth through the senses and observation (empiricism) and (b) the use of reason and logic (rationalism). Early proponents of Modernism divided themselves into two camps arguing which approach, empiricism or rationalism should take precedence. Modernists (rationalists) both in the sciences and religion tend to be more dogmatic and see things in terms of black and white.

(3) Postmodernism (1950s to present) - This is a reaction against the sometimes rigid dogmatism of Modernism. Postmodernism emphasizes the concept that there are many acceptable world views (pluralism) and many sources of truth, not just reason or observation.

Josh McDowell is an Evangelical apologist who has lectured on college campuses in defense of the existence of God since the 1960's. While driving back to New Jersey from Georgia I heard a radio interview with him in which he noted a fundamental shift in the challenges he heard from unbelievers regarding his lectures. In his first years of college lecturing, the primary challenge after giving a presentation was, "How do you know this is true? What proof do you have?" That was a modernist challenge. However, McDowell noted that during a very short period of time the usual challenge became something like, "Are you saying that Muslims and Jews are wrong? Don't you think that is arrogant?" This is a postmodernist challenge.

The Interaction Between Convictions and Mercy

The Modernist versus Postmodernist rivalry provides a twenty-first century context in which to view the differences between those who would give primary emphasis to conviction in religion and those who would stress mercy. However, the challenge of balancing conviction and mercy is nothing new. It is a historical struggle that has gone on from the beginnings of Christianity. Christ approved neither the looseness of the Sadducees nor the overemphasis on externals of the Pharisees. Paul battled those who emphasized salvation through the works of the law as well as those who said sarcastically, "Let us continue in sin that grace may abound."[4]

The truth, as will be pointed out in this book, is that both conviction, based on a common sense reading of the word of God, and mercy, based on God's character, are essential in imitating and serving him. They are not mutually exclusive, but rather should be inseparable companions. The tragedy today, however, is that many good people want to emphasize only one or the other, often correctly noticing the excesses of those who take the opposite side, while blithely oblivious to their own.

My perspective comes from many years living and working among those who want to be "just Christians." Though often called almost exclusively "churches of Christ," there is no official name in the scriptures to describe congregations that want to go back to basics in serving Christ without denominational affiliation. That goal has historically been a great challenge since denominational machinery and concepts are constantly making inroads. But, that's for another book on another occasion.

I suspect that some, especially those heavily influenced by Postmodernism or Evangelical thought may see much of the content of this book as "legalistic." Others who stress convictions with little emphasis on mercy may see parts of this book as not being harsh enough in dealing with error, especially if looking at them out of context. However, I strongly believe that developing both strong convictions and merciful attitudes are essential to imitating Christ. Either one without the other leads to spiritual disaster.

Questions and suggestions for thought

1. Ask Christians you know who are over fifty years old if they can give examples in their own experiences to illustrate the change from a Modernist/Rationalist approach to a Postmodern approach.

2. Think of conversations you have had with those who have a Postmodern approach to the Bible. ("It's all a matter of opinion," "One opinion is as good as another," etc.) Then, think of those you've had with those who take a more rational approach, who try to use reason, pin down definitions of words and analyze the context of scripture to determine truth. What are some differences in the way those two groups of people live? (Age? Occupation? General approach to life? How do these often differ?)

3. Who are some people you know who have been "taken captive" by philosophies of the world? Why has this always been a danger? What type of worldly philosophy might have the most influence on you?

4. Why might empty worldly philosophies have more influence on the masses now than in the past?

5. What can be done to combat them?

6. Why is it so easy to see how worldly philosophies have harmfully affected others, but so difficult to acknowledge how they are harmfully affecting us personally?

Thoughts for prayer: Pray specifically for young people (and older folks too!) who have been taken captive by worldly philosophies; for strength in not allowing them to harmfully affect us; for wisdom to avoid being caught up so much in the battles between worldly philosophies that we overreact and take our eyes off of Christ.

Chapter 2

Strengths and Weaknesses of a "Modernist" Approach to the Scriptures, Part 1

Pinning down definitions of words like "Modernism," especially in the context of religious thought is a challenge. It is used in a large number of different perspectives from art to history, politics and of course, religion. There almost seems to be as many definitions as writers. The term "rationalism" which often accompanies the term "Modernism" may be slightly easier to understand in a religious context. "In religion, rationalism is the view that recognizes as true only that content of faith that can be made to appeal to reason."[5]

Beginning in the 17th century, an influential group of European thinkers including Rene Descartes, Sir Frances Bacon and John Locke undermined the dominance of premodern thought and began the process of replacing it with modernist/rationalist thinking. They emphasized the use of reason in determining truth instead of unquestionably accepting the teaching of the Roman church. Bacon and Locke in particular believed in God and in using logic to discover divine truth from the scriptures. Almost simultaneously they emphasized the use of reason to discover scientific truth, believing that there was no contradiction between the two. Later, rationalist thinkers like Voltaire, began to reject scripture because some of it was unexplainable within their humanist context and therefore the term "rationalist" has come to be used almost exclusively in regards to non-believers.

A number of modern historians of the Stone-Campbell Restoration Movement are quick to point out the influence of rationalist thinkers, especially Sir Francis Bacon and John Locke on Alexander Campbell.

Locke's *The Reasonableness of Christianity* (1695) attempted to base Christianity on Baconian Inductive logic. It became the model for the next 150 years of moderately rationalist theology and was a favorite of Thomas and Alexander Campbell, who referred to Locke as the "Christian philosopher."[6]

Concerning Campbell, Bobby Valentine wrote,

He read *Letters on Toleration* and drank in Locke's concepts of religious liberty and toleration. In *Essays Concerning Human Understanding* and in Locke's empirical philosophy, a world of experiment, observation and reason, the young thinker found the basis of his method.... Campbell's basic epistemological position comes directly from Locke.[7]

Many of these historians consider this rationalist influence as a negative in the Restoration movement. They speak disparagingly of using a "CENI" (Command, Example, Necessary Inference) "hermeneutic" (method of interpreting the Bible). Though as will be pointed out, a hyper-rationalist approach to the scriptures can indeed take us away from Christ, the idea of using common sense in interpreting inspired scripture didn't originate with Sir Frances Bacon or John Locke but is found throughout the Bible. Searching for a divine precedent (for example, seeking command, example or necessary inference) is a practical approach to finding God's will, not a codified hermeneutic that originated in Europe in the late seventeenth century. God gave us common sense and expects us to use it!

Doy Moyer hit several nails squarely on the head with the following posts on Facebook.

We need to get past the constant criticism of CENI (Command, Example, Necessary Inference).

The problem with CENI is not that it is a failed hermeneutic. The problem is that we have clouded the terminology so much that we have forgotten what basic communication is all about. CENI is fancy talk for the basic principles of communication – what we use anywhere at any time for everyone. How so?

When you want to make your will known, how do you do it? May I suggest one of three ways? 1) You tell someone; 2) You show someone; 3) You imply something you expect people to get. This, of course, is the simplified version of CENI. When people disparage CENI, I don't think they've really thought this point through. Attacking CENI is attacking the foundation of communication. And it won't logically stand.

Here's the kicker: the whole principle (what I refer to more appropriately as "tell, show, and imply") is self-evident. Anyone who wants to deny this is free to try it. But if you do, please do not tell me anything about it, show me anything about it, or imply anything about it. To do so would be self-defeating.

In other words, "tell, show, and imply" is logically necessary. It is the way we communicate anything. Now I realize that this doesn't get to the nuts and bolts of application, but I do think we need to get past this constant criticism of CENI. Perhaps we should lose the CENI terminology, but the principle that underlies it is logically necessary. In my opinion, our mistake has been that we haven't explained that fundamental communication process—we've skipped right to the fancy talk and left people wondering, "where do you find that in the Bible?" You find it right where you find it anytime someone communicates anything. It is a fundamental starting point, and I don't believe anyone can logically deny it without defeating their own denial.[8]

Later he added, referring to CENI (command, example, necessary inference) in a simpler way as "tell, show, imply" (TSI).

Hermeneutics is the science of interpretation. It is what we as the recipients (readers, hearers) bring to the communication process. TSI, on the other hand, is inherent in what the communicator gives. That is, we, the readers or listeners, do not provide the TSI; we take the TSI that is given to us and try to understand what that means. TSI, then, is not a method of interpretation; it is the material that we try to interpret. We might misinterpret it. We might fail to get out of it what is intended. But it is nevertheless the raw material that we use in order to understand what the author or speaker intends. There is no getting around this. No one interprets anything that is not first told, shown, or implied.

So, CENI (TSI) is not a hermeneutic. It is the bare bones of what we work with when we do interpret. Thus, criticizing it as a failed hermeneutic is to misunderstand it at the most basic level. Instead of criticizing it, let's recognize it for what it is (inherent in the communication process) and then deal with how we should properly understand the statements, examples, and implications.[9]

Strengths of a Rationalist Approach to Faith

God's word was designed to be understood by humble people with common sense. Jesus praised the Father for that fact, "I praise you, Father, Lord of heaven and earth, that you have hidden these things from the wise and intelligent and have revealed them to infants. Yes, Father, for this way was well pleasing in your sight" (Matthew 11:25). Today, as in the first century, most theologians with their overcomplicated analysis miss fundamental truths about the teaching of Jesus that semiliterate farmers and laborers seem to grasp easily.

Jesus anticipated that his teaching could be understood with common sense.

• Matthew 7:21 - "Not everyone who says to me, 'Lord, Lord,' will enter the kingdom of heaven, but he who does the will of my Father who is in heaven wll enter."

• Matthew 7:24 – "Everyone then who hears these words of mine and acts on them..."

Jesus did not expect there would be any great confusion among truth seekers in understanding his will to do it. He assumed that truth seekers would understand his words and those of his inspired apostles and prophets and then choose to either to do them or not.

Jesus used traditional logic in Matthew 22:29-32 to confound the Sadducees. How could Jehovah be the God of Abraham, Isaac and Jacob and be the God of the living at the same time if they were not still alive in a very real sense?

Paul's letters are full of appeals to logic and reason. He expected such to be understood. Regarding his writings he said, "When you read this, you can perceive my insight into the mystery of Christ" (Ephesians 3:4). He told the Corinthians, "For we write nothing else to you than what you read and understand" (2 Corinthians 1:13).

After pointing out Israel's weakness in dealing with idolatry Paul pointed out that if we commune with Christ when partaking of the Lord's Supper, then we commune with idols when partaking of meat dedicated to them. However, he didn't come out and say it directly but expected the Corinthians to be able to judge for themselves on the basis of an inference. He wrote in 1 Corinthians 10:15,16, "I speak as to wise men; you judge what I say. Is not the cup of blessing which we bless a sharing in the blood of Christ? Is not the bread which we break a sharing in the body of Christ?"

Paul expected the Corinthians, who were not trained theologians, to come to the correct conclusion using common sense!

Christians today can be thankful to early religious "rationalists" who correctly pointed out that God's words weren't intended only for clergy but could generally be understood by sincere people of many different backgrounds.

Abuses of Scientific Rationalism

The dogmatism of scientific rationalists frustrates believers.
- Well, evolution is a theory. It is also a fact. And facts and theories are different things, not rungs in a hierarchy of increasing certainty. Facts are the world's data…. And humans evolved from ape-like ancestors whether they did so by Darwin's proposed mechanism or by some other yet to be discovered.[10] (Stephen Jay Gould)

- Creation science has not entered the curriculum for a reason so simple and so basic that we often forget to mention it: because it is false, and because good teachers understand exactly why it is false.[11] (Stephen Jay Gould)

- ...Anyone who denies the theory of evolution is either ignorant, stupid, insane, or wicked.[12] (Richard Dawkins)

Gould and other dogmatic evolutionists provide a classic example of all that can go wrong with Modernism. They have started with Charles Darwin and tried to patch all the leaky holes in his theory. Though they disagree among themselves about the various mechanisms needed to prop up their model, they try to present a façade of unanimity regarding its conclusions. Often, almost the only thing they have in common is a haughty disdain for anyone who would question what they want to be the final outcome—creation and design by nothing. The fact that they might need to go back and reassess some of their assumptions is unthinkable. In spite of numerous holes in the theory, dogmatic evolutionists have no qualms about making life miserable for others. They dismiss those who disagree with them as ignorant and try in every way possible to quarantine and gag them. Such dogmatic promoters of macro-evolution illustrate Modernism run amok. Something similar happens when religious rationalism runs amok.

Abuses of Spiritual Rationalism

Barton W. Stone was a young and promising Presbyterian preacher. After being moved by a revival in Southern Kentucky led by fellow Presbyterian, James McGreavy, he returned to his new home in Cane Ridge, Kentucky, near Paris, where another revival occurred in the summer of 1801.

However, Stone began to have doubts about the demands of his Presbyterian faith. The religion based its teaching on the *Westminster Confession of Faith*, a document designed to summarize the Bible's teaching in systematic form for Presbyterians. Stone's first doubts had to do with language concerning the Trinity.[13] At his ordination, he agreed to accept the confession, "as far as he saw it consistent with the word of God."[14]

Later he began to doubt the Calvinism in the *Westminster Confession of Faith*, especially the concept that the Holy Spirit works on the sinner apart from the word of God to effect conversion. Stone convinced several fellow preachers from the scriptures that sinners could believe the gospel and become Christians without the miraculous working of the Spirit.

When the Presbyterian Synod met in Lexington, Kentucky on September 6, 1803, most of the members were hostile to Stone for questioning the *Westminster Confession of Faith*. When Stone and his companions realized that they were going to be prosecuted and suspended, they instead withdrew themselves. They were forced to

> *"This is the most dangerous abuse of religious rationalism, giving the same importance to interpretation of God's word as to God's word itself."*

withdraw not on the basis of their attitude towards scripture, but on their loyalty to a human document designed to give a systematic summary of scripture. Thus a common sense approach to scripture had subtly been replaced by an insistence on acceptance of a codified human interpretation of scripture.

This is the most dangerous abuse of religious rationalism—giving the same importance to interpretation of God's word as to God's word itself. In such a case the interpretation becomes law on par with the law itself.

This was one of the great errors of the Pharisees, which Jesus combated in texts like Mark 7. There, the Pharisees and teachers of the law challenged Jesus because his disciples ate without washing their hands, thus violating the traditions of the elders. Though good for hygiene, hand washing before meals wasn't commanded under the law of Moses. However, the elders of the Jews extrapolated, perhaps from texts like Leviticus 15:11, 12 that if men should wash their hands and utensils under some circumstances, that to be safe, they should always wash them before eating. They then imposed that extrapolation as law.

Some of the strongest language in the New Testament can be found in the response of Jesus where he first quotes Isaiah 29:13 and then sums up the fact that the Pharisees were the object of that text.

> "This people honors me with their lips, but their heart is far from
> me; But in vain do they worship me, teaching as doctrines the
> precepts of men." Neglecting the commandment of God, you
> hold to the tradition of men. (Mark 7:6-8)

Binding systematic interpretations of men takes our mind away from our Creator and focuses it on human traditions.

Yes, interpretation is needed to analyze the scriptures. Some interpretations, usually those having to do with the funda-mentals, are practically self-evident (to use the language of the writers of the Declaration of Independence). Others, especially those regarding texts about deeper issues, require more analysis. The former might be considered "milk" and the latter "meat" (Hebrews 5:12). There are good interpretations, questionable interpretations, bad interpretations and off-the-wall interpreta-tions. The latter become prominent when people begin to be more concerned about defending their religious traditions or speculations rather than simply following Christ. The purer our motives are in simply wanting to follow Christ, the more correct our interpretations will be. The more we become con-cerned with maintaining a status quo or defending a cherished tradition, the more errors will creep into them.

Problems with bad interpretations multiply when they are systematized, bound upon groups of churches and used as a point of focus to determine truth. When such happens discussions as to how to obey God cease to center so much on the scriptures, but rather on the language of the systematized approach. People begin to appeal not to book, chapter or verse but rather to "Section I, paragraph B, number 2," "Page 41 of the workbook or magazine," "What Dungan's Hermeneutic says," "What brother so and so has taught," or "what we've always taught," etc. When that stage is reached, Christ and his inspired teaching are no longer the focus but rather the traditions of men. And thus we get into "creedalism."

Creedalism

Three hundred years after the birth of Christ, his followers had a number of challenges. One that they might have thought to be a blessing, acceptance by the Roman empire, was probably the greatest curse. Doctrinally, Arius, a popular preacher from Alexandria was gaining influence in his teaching that Christ was a created being. "There was (once) when Christ was not."[15] His teaching affected his influential friend, Eusebius of Caesarea and others of note.

By this time, however, a power structure in the church had been sufficiently developed to do something about the influence of Arius on an empire-wide scale. Bishops found an ally in the emperor Constantine, who though understanding little about the issues involved, was eager to use his influence to help. He invited the bishops to his royal palace in Nicea in May of the year 325 to work out the problem.[16]

The solution that the bishops sought was a creed, a statement of faith that could define orthodoxy for the church, considered by the leaders to be those under the control of the bishops. The result was the Nicene Creed, a document designed to uphold the deity of Christ while condemning (anathematizing) all who made statements that might undermine it.

At the first glance, the Nicene Creed might be seen as a positive way of dealing with a pesky and dangerous heresy. However, in several ways it set a dangerous precedent:

1. It set up a document of human interpretation on par with God's law.

2. It took a prerogative that belongs only to God, pronouncing condemnation, and put it in hands of men, "the church."

Since the precedent set at Nicea, the Catholic church has added a number of creeds, each codifying the prevailing thoughts of the bishops of the time and pronouncing anathemas on any who would challenge them. Protestantism has followed the lead. Each of the mainstream denominations has taken upon itself the authority to produce written creeds to encapsulate their interpretations and making rules that must be followed to be considered faithful members. Even disciples who consider themselves nonsectarian are often tempted to create unwritten creeds, official interpretations accepted by a network of churches that begin to be referenced on a par with scripture when determining how to proceed.

Denominationalism

A logical result of creedalism is denominationalism that results when all who agree upon a creed, written or unwritten, lump themselves together, viewing the network that they have formed as "the right church." Biblically, God's church is simply all saved individuals known to him (Acts 20:28; Hebrews 12:28). However, as denominations form they often begin to look upon God's church as a network of congregations (and eventually the institutions belonging to the network) that accepts the human creed.

Traditional denominations - The traditional denominations usually began with a founder like Martin Luther (Lutheranism), John Calvin (whose disciple John Knox is credited with starting the Presbyterian church), John Wesley (Methodism), etc. These founders developed a systematic approach to the scriptures (found in written creeds) that attracts followers who are loyal to the system.

As progressive approaches to the scriptures have become increasingly influential, mainstream denominations no longer look upon themselves as the right church of God, but rather as a tradition within God's church. Differences between them have come to be considered almost completely irrelevant. The thought of an energetic debate between a Lutheran and a Methodist would be almost unimaginable now because differences between the two groups would be considered unimportant. Thus, ecumenism, the union of churches in spite of differences, has been in vogue for the past one hundred years, although the loss of convictions in most has resulted in plummeting numbers and influence.

"Non-denominational" denominations - Efforts to get away from the human creeds and dogma of traditional denominationalism have seldom been successful for more than two or three generations, because the children, grandchildren and great grandchildren of those who originally pull away from them eventually form their own. Occasionally, even some of the first generation succumb. For example, Alexander Campbell, who originally taught the need to get away from denominationalism, when he became prosperous and famous promoted the support of denominational machinery that eventually became a part of the Disciples of Christ denomination.

Christians influenced by men like David Lipscomb and F.B. Syrgley, who fought the denominationalism of the "Disciples of Christ" began to form their own "Church of Christ" denomination. They ceased thinking of God's church as simply all the saved to whom God would extend His mercy, and began to consider it to be a network of churches that they could define, at least in their minds, with church directories. The controversy over institutionalism in the 1950's and 1960's had to do with this primary issue, What is God's church? Though cloaked in arguments about the use of the church treasury and whether a congregation could send $25 a month to an orphans' home, the fundamental issue, at least in the minds of the most perceptive, was whether God's church was a network of congregations that should have such denominational machinery or simply saved individuals known only to God.

Among those described by historians as "noninstitutional" there should be a constant reanalysis to avoid the concept that God's church is a network of congregations that has its "unofficial" schools and traditions. Biblically it is simply all those who are saved as they go through of various levels of spiritual growth (Heb. 12:23; Acts 20:28).

Questions for thought

1. Does it really matter what people several hundred years ago thought about how to arrive at truth? However, can seeing their thinking help us to avoid their errors and gain perspective?

2. Why is the concept that God would give us vague instructions about how to serve him so harmful?

3. Talk about other scriptural references other than those given here where inspired writers and teachers showed that they expected their words to be generally understood.

4. Why are humble people often able to understand scriptural principles better than "scholars?" Why do you think God wanted it that way? What are some dangers of too much emphasis on scholarship?

5. Have you ever had experiences with dogmatic evolutionists or atheists, perhaps college professors? Have you ever talked to anyone about the Bible who showed similar attitudes?

6. What is the difference between expressing a conviction about Bible teaching, and binding a human creed on others? (This will take a lot of thought!)

7. Why is there such a strong tendency in men to want to see God's church as a network of congregations or an historical movement rather than saved individuals?

Thoughts for prayer: For help to have the complete submission to God that is necessary to take his word as little children, at face value; for honesty to fight the tendency to look upon the scriptures as something to support human traditions and agendas or create written or unwritten creeds; for wisdom to avoid seeing his church as a network of local congregations or as a historical movement, but rather as saved individuals.

Chapter 3

Strengths and Weaknesses of a "Modernist" Approach to the Scriptures, Part 2

Disregarding Mercy

The brother who walked up to the pulpit in Eastern Kentucky was an experienced debater in the mountain tradition. He could make his followers laugh at his sarcastic plays on words and little rejoinders designed to make his opponent look foolish. It's not that he wasn't sincere. He was very honest in his conviction that 1 Corinthians 14:34 and 1 Timothy 2:11, 12 prohibited women from asking a question in any kind of Bible study as well as from teaching a group of children or other women. The sarcastic debating style was all he knew and he was very good at it.

Before starting the first speech, he looked out confidently over the audience that was composed primarily of his sympathizers and began to speak with a booming voice that easily overpowered the noisy air conditioner in the back of the small building.

"One of us," he said deliberately, "is going to hell. Either my opponent is going to hell or I am going to hell!"

With those words, the tone of the debate was set and the two contestants went after each other. After about thirty seconds of his first speech it became quite apparent that he didn't think that he was the one who was going to hell!

The debating brother from Eastern Kentucky spoke as if he had absolutely no concept of God's patience or mercy in dealing with those are seeking him. This is a common attitude among those who don't consider the mercy of Jesus.

Richard Hughes told of a hard-line preacher in the 1930's who preached four sermons in a congregation in Cincinnati, Ohio that were "forceful" but "largely pugnacious." F.L. Rowe then asked him to preach a sermon on the Prodigal Son. The preacher hesitated a minute and then said, "Brother Rowe, I cannot do it. I have never studied the subject."[17]

Those who have very little concept of mercy often allow their exchanges over religious differences to deteriorate to sarcastic queries as to whether those who disagree will "go to hell." Unfortunately discussions of difficult texts like 1 Corinthians 11:2-16 often seem to quickly reach this level, "Do you mean to tell me that every woman who doesn't wear a hat to services is going to hell?" Just yesterday as I write, I observed an exchange over baptism for the remission of sins on Facebook that quickly deteriorated to challenges about who was going to the final abode of the wicked.

For hyper-rationalists, all scriptures are so easy to understand, that even fools "could not err therein" (Isaiah 35:8 KJV). They apply that prophesy even to difficult texts like 1 Corinthians 11:2-16, ignoring other passages like 2 Peter 3:16 which refers to the difficulty of understanding some of Paul's writings. Therefore if someone disagrees with them, even on difficult issues like the covering when praying, it's because they're just plain stubborn and don't love the truth.

While such characterizations might be true in some circumstances, scriptures speak continually about God's patience and mercy with those seeking him and growing in their understanding of his will. Yes, he punishes those who are blatantly disobedient towards his authority or who reach a point in their rebellion where no reconciliation is possible (Israel's captivity, Nadab and Abihu, Ananias and Saphira, etc.). However he is "merciful and gracious, slow to anger and abounding in steadfast love and faithfulness" (Ps. 86:15) when his followers are seeking him with a penitent heart, though they are often clumsy in their efforts.

• He did not choose to have David stoned for his adultery,[18] though that was the prescribed punishment for the act (Lev. 20:10-12).

• He chose not to punish some of the remnants of the Northern ten tribes when they presumptuously ate the Passover without washing themselves (2 Chronicles 30:18-20).

• The Psalmist says in Psalm 103, God "has not dealt with us according to our sins, Nor rewarded us according to our iniquities.… For He Himself knows our frame; He is mindful that we are but dust." (verses 10, 14).

Hyper-rationalists like our brother from Eastern Kentucky and the brother who had never studied the story of the Prodigal Son are oblivious to such expressions of grace and mercy in the scriptures.

Sometimes brethren overly affected by currents like Postmodernism complain that abrasive conservatives give too much importance to the scriptures. Some have even invented the word "bibliolatry" to characterize the attitudes of those they feel to be too concerned about biblical authority.[19] The problem with overly harsh "conservatives" is not that they give too much importance to the scriptures, but rather that they don't give enough importance to them—in particular the passages that emphasize grace and mercy! They pick and choose texts that emphasize punishment and blithely overlook those balancing texts about clemency.

Paul gives a key to showing mercy in Philippians 4:5—"Let your gentle *spirit* be known to all men. The Lord is near." The word "gentle" in this text is also used in 2 Corinthians 10:1 to describe the way Paul wanted to approach the Corinthians, "with the gentleness of Christ." A.T Robertson says of the word, "Courtesy is not far from the true idea. It is graciousness with strength and poise of character." L.A. Mott says in *Thinking Through Philippians*, "The adjective is contrasted with the battling, contentious disposition" (p. 100). According to the last part of verse 5, the gentleness comes from the awareness that the Lord is near. An awareness of the Father's closeness must have helped Jesus on the Cross where though reviled, "...did not revile in return; while suffering, He uttered no threats, but kept entrusting Himself to Him who judges righteously" (1 Peter 2:23). Harsh and merciless brethren are completely oblivious to these Biblical principles.

The System Becomes Law

Should congregations allow singing during the Lord's Supper?

"Absolutely not!" said the godly Christian woman. "There is no authority to mix any of the five acts of worship!" she said decisively.

I agreed with the sister that singing during the Lord's Supper is intrusive. There is much emphasis given to silence in the scriptures for reflection and thought,[20] but our noise crazed society has to have some kind of sound, even during the reflective moments of the breaking of bread. What grabbed my attention however was the rule to which she appealed—"there is no authority for mixing any of the five acts of worship." There are at least two problems with this "hyper-rationalist" approach:

(1) Nowhere in the scriptures is worship divided into five distinct categories: Lord's Supper, offering, singing, prayer and exhortation or teaching. That is an arbitrary categorization that if presented as such is harmless. However, as tends to happen with hyper-rationalists, it has become a law and a checklist in the minds of many good people. It becomes an unwritten creed! They overlook the fact that the way we worship God when coming together could be divided into a number of other scriptural categories, for example: praise, supplication, giving of thanks, exhortation, reproof, instruction, singing psalms, singing hymns, scripture reading, partaking of bread, partaking of the cup, etc. Those who know the scriptures know the references that could be given for all the previously mentioned "acts."

(2) The scriptures often mix different types of worship. Many of the Psalms which were songs were also prayers. Such is the case of many hymns we sing today, for example, "More Holiness Give Me." Hymns like "Yield Not to Temptation" are hymns of exhortation, taking into account that as we sing, we "teach and exhort each other."[21] Sounds like mixing to me.

The rule created in the mind of the good sister that "there's no authority to mix the five acts of worship," sounded reasonable and might have convinced some. However, it was an overreach, a sometimes unhealthy consequence of hyper-rationalism.

Traditionalism

An evangelist in a town in the Northeast managed to find a few Christians in the area and decided to start a new congregation. At the first service a woman who had been a Christian for a number of years in Alabama appeared agitated. When asked why, she responded, "We can't partake of the Lord's Supper using that table. It doesn't have the words, 'Do this in memory of me' engraved on the front." For all of her life she had partaken of the bread and fruit of the vine that had been placed on a table with those engraved words. Something was just plain wrong in her mind about partaking now from a table without those words.

There is sometimes a difference of judgment among faithful Christians about what should go on the church's sign. If all

> *"...This issue can quickly deteriorate into ungodly wrangling when argued from a traditionalist point of view on one hand or a rebellious attitude on the other."*

proposed designations can be defended with scripture, this is a matter of judgment and when treated as such causes no harm. An argument can be made that travelers are accustomed to the term "church of Christ" when seeking congregations that want to restore first century principles taught by Christ's inspired apostles. However, an equally good argument can be made that a "Church of Christ" denomination now exists and that it would be good to disassociate from that denomination by putting something like "Christians meet here," or "the Lord's church" on a church's sign.

Unfortunately, however, this issue can quickly deteriorate into ungodly wrangling when argued from a traditionalist point of view on one hand or a rebellious attitude on the other. One traditional disciple sarcastically asked someone defending an untraditional sign if he was "ashamed of the 'Church of Christ.'" The second brother quickly asked his questioner if he was "ashamed of the church of God," correctly pointing out with that simple follow-up question the sectarian concepts revealed in the question. The original questioner didn't have a good answer.

However, I'm afraid there is a grain of truth in the fear that some, though not all, who object to using the term "church of Christ" on signs, not only want to disassociate themselves from the denomination that uses that name, but also from practices that come not from the denomination but from Christ—for example, baptism for the remission of sin, simple worship that avoids entertainment-oriented elements, etc.

Good reasons can be given for the practice of putting "Church of Christ" on the church's sign. However, to impose an unwritten law or creed to that effect is traditional sectarianism at its worst, since the scriptures specify no such designation, but rather refer to God's people in a number of different ways.

Another similar issue regards dress when attending worship services on the first day of the week. When left as a matter of opinion or judgment, it doesn't have to cause problems. Traditionally, Christians have worn their "Sunday best" to worship gatherings on Sunday, though more casual wear has usually been worn for services during the week. Some reason persuasively that our dress reflects how much importance we give to an activity. To go to court, for example, in blue jeans and a tee shirt, would reveal a lack of respect for the solemnity and authority of the occasion. The same, it is argued, would be true of wearing similar clothing to partake of the Lord's Supper with the saints.

Others point out that ties were certainly not worn in the first century and that to make a kind of "fashion show" out of worship assemblies is an abuse and could make those of the highways and byways uncomfortable when they visit us.

I lean a little towards the first position, but acknowledge that it can be taken to an extreme. I have seen an over emphasis on dress in some places. What is wrong would be making a law that you cannot attend services without a tie. That would be traditionalism that comes from hyper-rationalism.

"Issue-oriented Congregations"

I talked once with a brother about a congregation that constantly had problems with various brotherhood issues. He remarked, "That's an issue-oriented congregation." That description grabbed my attention. Should a congregation be oriented primarily to issues? Or, should it be oriented to a person, Jesus Christ? Is it possible to be so oriented to issues, even important issues, that we can begin to take a little focus off of Christ, who he is, his sacrifice, his love and grace, etcetera?

My father told about talking with an impressive young woman who had become a Christian about two years earlier. She said something like this—"I've been taught about Bible authority, the church, denominationalism and the difference between the Old Testament and the New Testament. You know what I would like to study now? I would like to study about Jesus!"

The church at Ephesus was well taught about issues that affected congregations of its time such as the doctrine of the Nicolaitans and false apostles who were wandering around Asia, but God was at the point of rejecting it because it had "left its first love" (Rev. 2:4). In the same way, congregations today can become very well taught on issues of the day like instrumental music, institutionalism and liberalism in general and still be in danger of losing their candlestick because they've lost their first love.

I'm sometimes asked, "Is that a sound congregation?" Twenty-five years ago that question meant, "Does it reject church support of institutionalism?" Or perhaps, "Is it well taught regarding the 'new hermeneutic?'" Almost never am I asked, "Is that congregation sound in love or prayer?" It is so easy to be an issue-oriented congregation, to the neglect of being a Christ-oriented congregation.

Of course, if a congregation is totally dedicated to Christ, it is going to educate itself regarding issues and dangerous doctrines that may threaten that focus. The churches at Pergamus and Thyatira were condemned because of their lackadaisical attitudes towards the doctrines of the Nicolaitans and Balaam (Rev. 2:14,15; 10-15). However, our primary focus as congregations of the Lord should not be upon various issues of the day with a secondary focus upon Jesus Christ as the Son of God, but rather the other way around. May God help us to focus primarily on his Son, and as a result of that love for him, may he help us to educate ourselves about issues that may affect that relationship.

Problems Caused by Hyper-rationalism Among Others

Garrison Keilor has become a kind of pop-philosopher through his weekly *Prairie Home Companion* show on National Public Radio. In an early book, "Lake Wobegon Days," he described life among the Plymouth Free Brethren of his youth.

> In a town where everyone was either Lutheran or Catholic, we were neither one. We were 'exclusive' Brethren, a branch that believed in keeping itself pure of false doctrine by avoid-

ing association with the impure. Some Brethren assemblies, mostly in the larger cities, were not so strict and broke bread with strangers – we referred to them as 'the so-called Open Brethren'... whereas we made sure that any who fellowshipped with us were straight on all details of the Faith, as set forth by the first brethren who left the Anglican Church in 1865 to worship on the basis of correct principles...

Unfortunately, once free of the worldly Anglicans, these firebrands were not content to worship in peace but turned their guns on each other. Scholarly to the core and perfect literalists every one, they set to arguing over points that, to an outsider, would have seemed very minor indeed but which to them were crucial to the Faith, including the question: if Believer A is associated with Believer B who has somehow associated himself with C who holds a False Doctrine, must A break off association with B, even though B does not hold the Doctrine, to avoid the taint?

The correct answer is: Yes....

Once having tasted the pleasure of being Correct and defending True Doctrine, they kept right on and broke up at every opportunity, until by the time I came along, there were dozens of tiny Brethren groups, none of which were speaking to any of the others.[22]

Keilor's analysis sums up some of the basic problems among the Plymouth Free Brethren that appeared when convictions were emphasized without mercy, in particular, a weakening fragmentation. (Reading the history of the Plymouth Free Brethren shows many parallels between that movement and the Stone-Campbell Restoration Movement.) It is sometimes easier to acknowledge such problems when looking at others, but those influenced by the Restoration Movement would be foolish to act as if such were unknown among us. If we're honest, most of us must admit knowing of places where the preaching of the ancient gospel has been greatly hindered by proud, know-it-all "Church of Christers" who have been quick to argue but either slow or completely unwilling to humbly serve others in their communities. Emphasizing conviction without mercy, they have become odious to those around them and churches where they have dominated have either fragmented or died. They are the opposite of every word James used to describe the wisdom from above: "first pure, then peaceable, gentle, reasonable, full of mercy and good fruits, unwavering, without hypocrisy" (James 3:17).

I am thankful for those in my youth who showed me that conviction and mercy don't have to be incompatible. My grandfather, Gardner Hall Sr., mixed his strong, conservative convictions with an emphasis on God's mercy and grace. Irven Lee doggedly fought the denominational machinery that was pushed so aggressively among known congregations in North Alabama in the 1950's and 1960's but always with a kind and gentlemanly spirit that increased his effectiveness. Bennie Lee Fudge was also an effective evangelist who successfully merged conviction and mercy. They were "first pure, then peaceable, gentle, reasonable, full of mercy and good fruits, unwavering, without hypocrisy."

May God help us to put into practice all the New Testament principles, not only those that deal with acts of worship and organization, but also those that instruct us to be humble and merciful. May the cocky, strutting, arrogant, in-your-face, "Church of Christer" disappear forever.

Questions for thought

1. Have you ever known preachers who would have a difficult time presenting a lesson on the Prodigal Son or God's Mercy?

Have you ever known any that might have difficulty giving a lesson on eternal punishment? Why would both be wrong?

2. Why do you think people sometimes quickly want to ask those who take various positions if others that disagree with them are going to hell? Is this question designed to help determine truth? Or to put someone on the defensive?

3. What are some texts about mercy and the importance of avoiding carnal disputes that contentious brethren overlook? When thinking of such texts, is their problem giving too much emphasis to Bible teaching, or too little?

4. Are unsound reasons sometimes given to back up important points? Why is such generally not helpful?

5. Why is it such a danger to become so issue oriented that little emphasis is given to the person of Jesus Christ? Why is it so easy for this to happen?

6. What issues come to your mind when you hear the term "sound congregation?" Why might some adjustments need to be made to that concept?

7. Why is church fragmentation such a triumph for Satan?

Thoughts for prayer: For a merciful yet firm spirit in dealing with others; for the desire to seek truth above personal victories and then help people see truth rather than win carnal victories over them; for forgiveness for sometimes trying to win carnal victories rather than humbly seek truth; for God's mercy.

Chapter 4

The Rebellion Against Modernism/Rationalism

R evolutionary approaches in thinking often reflect
rebellion against the abuses of the establishment
and such is the case with religious antirationlism.
Though the Postmodern tendency to underemphasize
convictions has done much harm, it would be foolish not
to acknowledge some areas in which it is reacting against
very real abuses.

Anti-Pharisaism

Jesus hated Pharisaism! Though correct in rejecting the mixing
of Greek ideas with principles of God's law and in combating the excesses of the liberal Sadducees, Pharisees allowed
themselves to drift away from God in a number of areas and
drag others with them to perdition. Pharisaism had several
distinct errors that were criticized by Jesus:

1. An overemphasis on externals and corresponding lack
of concern for the heart and inner holiness (Matthew
23:23).

2. A desire to make a hedge around the law by binding interpretations that they made to protect it (Mark 7:5-7).

3. Pride and self-sufficiency (Matthew 23).

The label "Pharisee" is often unfairly used in personal attacks against anyone who is "conservative." Jesus never condemned the Pharisees, however, for their strict-construction approach to interpreting the scriptures, but rather for their corrupt heart that revealed itself through their many inconsistencies. Though the word is often used unfairly and disparagingly, we would be foolish to act as if elements of Pharisaism weren't a danger to God's people today.

Henry Kriete was a member of the International Church of Christ (known before as "the Boston Movement") in London, England. In 2003 he wrote an eloquent open letter to the leadership of the International Church of Christ, which had a devastating effect on that denominational system and was one of the main catalysts in its reorganization. His section on Pharisaism is one of the most moving descriptions of that danger that I've ever read. I will quote below large portions of that article which can be found online (http://www.reveal. org/library/stories/people/hkriete.htm).

> The Pharisees, or "the separate ones," had misguided but noble intentions to begin with. They wanted to protect the law from law-breakers and so imposed a religious system of rules and regulations and traditions to be a "hedge" around the law of God. They reasoned: "If they don't break our rules, then they will not be able to break the Law of Moses." We all know this. And we all know the sorry outcome– freedom denied, individual integrity diminished, the Sabbath becomes a tyranny, the weightier matters of the law-justice, love and mercy– neglected, and ultimately, the eventual slavery of men to the powers that be.

Once their religious system was firmly established, it then only needed to be stabilized and maintained. Over time, naturally, the Pharisees as an institution became systemically evil. Therefore, what they came to represent "as a whole"– what they evolved into, needed to be exposed and vigorously denounced by Christ. What an offence that must have been! In fact, has the world ever witnessed such a sustained and unsparing attack on religious leaders? I don't think so.

Certainly, there must have been sincere Pharisees, Paul for one. And a few more we can assume from reading the gospels. But together-as a system of religious authority – they were "sons of hell," "fools," "blind guides," "whitewashed tombs," "a brood of vipers." and finally, a barrier to the truth of God's goodness and grace: "You shut the kingdom of heaven in men's faces." They were lawyers and teachers of the law; sharp and prominent and well respected (at least to their face). They sat "in Moses' seat" and so needed to be "obeyed." They were men of extreme dedication and zeal - missionaries to distant countries and fanatically "separate"' from all outward sins. Nevertheless, in spite of their sincerity and zeal for God, every convert to the Pharisees in the words of Jesus, became "twice as much a son of hell" as the one who converted them. That is how powerful a religious system can be. It will ignore the voice of conscience, the voice of reason and even the voice of God.

In light of this, should we as leaders not pause to reflect on our own leadership values and doctrines? Should we not humble ourselves, and even tremble before God when we realize how extensive this battle between Christ and the religious leaders of his day became? Why such rigorous denunciations and warnings? Why so many written heated exchanges in the gospels? Why would Jesus - who was meek and lowly - publicly berate them and insult them and constantly expose their hypocrisies to public shame? My answer is this-they were to be an example and warning to you and me, the religious leaders of our own generation. This demonic tendency towards pride and control, ostracization and greed, no matter what name it goes by or in what century, will keep on waging war until it has once again infiltrated and ruined the integrity of God's leaders. And through us, into the church.

Many young disciples today, though sometimes overreacting, are right to oppose elements of Pharisaism that are very real dangers.

Anti Denominationalism

Traditional denominations are losing members in droves. Since 1960 the Episcopalian Church has lost 32.6% of it's membership, the United Methodist church is down 23.6%, the Presbyterian Church USA is down 21.1%.[23] The numbers behind the decline are even more impressive when counting the number of members per 1000 inhabitants as the population grows.

The primary reason for the decline in mainstream denominations is probably their loss of conviction. Perhaps a secondary reason is that those influenced by Postmodernism hate human creeds and traditions and therefore leave the denominations where creeds and human traditions have been emphasized. That is a good thing!

Churches that are growing are usually independent groups led by dynamic preachers. I often hear people refer to those from such independent churches as "denominational" but such couldn't be further from the truth. Their problem isn't traditional denominationalism in the sense of wanting to belong to some kind of a worldwide religious organization, but rather there is often an infatuation with entertainment-oriented worship, a tendency to elevate the "pastor" who becomes almost like a celebrity and an emphasis on feelings over scriptural substance.

Young disciples influenced by Postmodernism often oppose denominational concepts among known churches of Christ. They should be applauded and supported in such opposition. A young man who is struggling spiritually told me about his aversion to denominational attitudes he sees among his brethren. Though I think he has greater spiritual challenges than the mistaken concepts of his brethren and that he exaggerates a bit, he has noticed a kind of old boy's network that does smack sometimes of denominationalism. He wrote,

> I have come to believe that the church of Christ is simply a social circle, just like any other denominational church. "Tom knows Dick whose son is the cousin of the preacher in Bugtussle and went to college with me." ...We boast about not being a denomination but almost everyone I know considers the church of Christ to be a denomination. It has its own college, its own lectures, its own camps, etc.... The college has a Biblical study program to create preachers that are then sent to internships at various churches of Christ.

I responded that early Christians knew each other and recommended each other (Romans chapter 16) and that it's not wrong for groups of Christians to teach others in various settings without being a denomination. And yet as I made those points with him, I had to acknowledge that some seem to have the concept of the church of Christ as a kind of social circle or network of local congregations and also that there is sometimes a boasting, party spirit among some. That fact doesn't justify neglecting the Lord's Supper or participating in entertainment-oriented worship where other Biblical truths are ignored, but it does discourage many young people.

Another spiritual benefit that has come from the rejection of hyper-rationalism by many young disciples is the waning influence of the big preacher or "editor bishops." For better or worse, many in my parents' and grandparents' generations were in awe of famous preachers. Around the turn of the 19th century godly men like David Lipscomb and T.B. Larimore became household names among disciples. In the 1930's and 1940's Foy E. Wallace could make those who disagreed with him tremble. Others who exerted great influence in the 1930's and 1940' were N. B. Hardeman and G.C. Brewer. In the 1950's and 1960's men like B.C. Goodpasture, Guy N. Woods, Roy Cogdill, Gus Nichols and others were very famous. Many who admired them would say things like "whatever brother ____ says is what I believe!" Though many of those men deserved respect and appreciation, the adulation often went too far! After all, they were men. Thankfully, that type of idolization is becoming increasingly rare.

Willingness to Reassess Suppositions

Francis Chan is an impressive Evangelical preacher who has written two popular books, *Crazy Love* and *Forgotten God, Our Tragic Neglect of the Holy Spirit*. Though the books have some flaws that will be discussed later, Chan himself has many admirable qualities. I'm not sure how much he may have been influenced by Postmodernism. On one hand, he reasons from the scriptures. On the other, he seems to accept that the Holy Spirit speaks to us apart from the word through hunches and circumstances in our lives and flat out states that he doesn't rule out modern day revelation (*Forgotten God*, p. 55). Such reliance on subjective sources of revelation is one of the biggest flaws among those who claim to be Christians and have been influenced by Postmodernism. One thing that impresses me about Chan, however, is his willingness to reassess some traditional Evangelical teaching, for example on baptism.

When answering the question as to whether baptism saves or not on *Youtube*,[24] he went directly to 1 Peter 3:20, 21 and analyzed it correctly. He then alluded to Romans 6:3,4 pointing out that we are baptized into Christ and "into his salvation, into his sacrifice and everything he's done for us." He said, "God never says in there that if you want to follow me to raise your hand, walk down an aisle and say a prayer. What he prescribes is repent and be baptized." These statements are biblical, but would never be made by traditional Evangelicals.

Of course, we might justifiably question whether Chan lives consistently with this truth, since he seems to receive as faithful those who stubbornly refuse to accept it. In fact in his book, *Crazy Love*, he tells of preaching a funeral sermon where there were "at least two hundred students at the front of the church praying for salvation" (p. 49). So which is it? "God never says" that for salvation you must "walk down the aisle and say a prayer?" Or, "at least two hundred... praying for salvation?" Perhaps Chan is still working these issues out in his mind and is moving towards the truth. I would hope that in the future if there were two hundred people praying for salvation he would simply tell them to do what Peter told those in the day of Pentecost to do, and what he acknowledged in the video is necessary, repentance and baptism. That's not traditional Evangelical teaching, but it's truth. I doubt that any traditional Protestant, raised on the systematic theology of Calvin or Wesley, would ever make such statements as Chan has made. Chan's laudable willingness to reanalyze the purpose of baptism reflects one of the good sides of anti-rationalism, a willingness to reassess traditions.

Though those of us who have been influenced by the Stone-Campbell Restoration movement are happy to see young people reassess old Evangelical or Catholic traditions, we get nervous and sometimes overreact when younger Christians want to reanalyze old cherished doctrines among known churches of Christ. Of course, when this reassessment is done with a spirit of rebellion, as is sometimes the case, there's cause for concern. Often, however, young disciples simply want to "Test all things; hold fast what is good" (1 Thessalonians 5:22 NKJV), and they should be encouraged in such investigations. It does young disciples no good to simply accept something because they have heard it from their parents. As the old saying goes, "truth has nothing to fear." Or, as John Milton put it,

> Though all the winds of doctrine were let loose to play upon the earth, so Truth be in the field, we do injuriously by licensing and prohibiting to misdoubt her strength. Let her and Falsehood grapple; who ever knew Truth put to the worse, in a free and open encounter.[25]

Thought questions

1. Why is Pharisaism (a prideful and almost exclusive emphasis on externals) such a subtle danger?

2. How can the term "Pharisee" be used unfairly as an epithet?

3. What are some ways that those who claim to be undenominational can gradually come to have the party spirit ("Our group's the right one!") and party pride that is characteristic of denominationalism?

4. What are some examples of party pride (pride in "our network of churches" more than confidence in God) that you have seen in others? When might you have seen some party pride in yourself?

5. Have you seen some examples of people who seem refreshingly willing to reanalyze some of their cherished traditions?

How willing are you to reanalyze some beliefs that you have had for years?

6. What are some differences between those who reanalyze beliefs because of a spirit of resentment and rebellion, and those who do so for a love of truth? Why are these differences so important?

Thoughts for prayer: For help in avoiding the unhealthy aspects of Pharisaism; forgiveness for party pride and help in avoiding the tendency to identify with a movement or network of churches more than with Christ and his body of saved individuals; for the love of the truth which will help us constantly analyze our beliefs, not with a spirit of rebellion against our parents or others, but because we love God.

Chapter 5

Spiritual Problems with Antirationalism/Postmodernism

(1) A De-emphasis on Words, Language

He "will tell you words by which you and all your household will be saved" (Acts 14:22 NKJV).

Words are of fundamental importance in Christ's system of faith. The gospel (revealed in words) is the power of God to salvation (Romans 1:16). God chose to save the world by the "foolishness of preaching" (1 Cor. 1:21 KJV). We are called by the gospel (2 Thess. 2:13). God manifested his hope of eternal life in his word through the preaching of Paul and others (Titus 1:3, ESV). Every case of conversion in the book of Acts is preceded by the preaching of the good news about Jesus. The sword of the Spirit is the Word of God (Eph. 6:17). This is one of the areas in which Postmodernism clashes with the sword of the Spirit.

One of the first recognized Postmodern philosophers, Jean-François Lyotard, used the term "metanarratives" to refer to the language of legal, social, political and religious institutions,[26] affirming that they involved "language games"[27] that were used to try to oppress others. While perhaps true in some settings (I think of Marxism, feminism and other "isms"), Lyotard attacked the idea that any rational understanding at all could be gained from words since such were subject to multiple interpretations. Critics have pointed out that if all metanarratives should be considered language games, then his writings should be considered such! Lyotard seemed to acknowledge this at least in part, "every utterance should be thought of as a 'move' in a game."[28] A contemporary of Lyotard, Michel Foucault, "was known for his controversial aphorisms such as 'language is oppression.'"[29] I believe that the phrase, "language is oppression," is oppressive!

Though most who claim to follow Jesus would reject the extremes of such French philosophers, it would be naive to think that their way of thinking has had no impact on us. The tendency to de-emphasize words as a way to knowing God, while emphasizing feelings and personal experience is very much in style in Evangelical circles. Postmodernism has had its effect!

There are several ways that some who have been influenced by Postmodernism try to undermine the confidence and importance of words in the New Testament:

(a) **Questioning translations** - A sister in Christ sent my wife an article written by a preacher in a noninstitutional congregation, questioning whether we can really come to know truth because there are so many different translations. It seemed that the purpose of the piece was to undermine confidence in the importance of Biblical words.

It is true that most of us have to rely upon translations of God's word and that some are more accurate than others. It is also true that some idiomatic expressions and local flavors may be better understood if one has a knowledge of the ancient languages of the Scriptures. However, one of the great strengths of the Bible is that good translations give the same powerful message as that given in the original languages of the Bible. God's plan for man and our need to respond to it come through loud and clear through any number of good Bible translations. No great Biblical doctrine is put in doubt by differences in any of the good ones.

(b) Questioning the composition of the New Testament canon
Another method used to undermine trust in the written word is to question the canon, the list of accepted inspired books of New Testament. Though some question whether some books of the Old Testament Apocrypha should be included in the Bible, the efforts to cast doubt on the twenty-seven books of the New Testament are even more dangerous. Though this is not a place for a deep analysis of the issue, a few short points might be helpful.

Determining which books have the high standards of inspiration and which don't, doesn't depend primarily on analyzing the opinions of second and third century disciples regarding the issue. While we admire their caution, we can determine even today which writings come from the Holy Spirit and which don't. For example, there are a few ancient texts that according to a very few should be considered as inspired writings in addition to the 27 traditional books. The most commonly mentioned candidate is the Gospel of Thomas. My challenge to any who wonder if books like the Gospel of Thomas should be included in the canon is simply to read them. The superiority of New Testament books will quickly become apparent. That comes from the fact that they were inspired! Books like the Gospel of Thomas were not.

(c) Questioning the gradual formation of the canon over a hundred years after Christ's death. Another tactic used by those influenced by Postmodernism to undermine the concept of seeking Bible authority is to point out that many New Testament books weren't available to many Christians until the end of the second century at the earliest and possibly later than that. They ask, "How can you say that you're imitating early Christians by demanding 'book, chapter and verse,' when they didn't even have the New Testament?"

The answer of course, is that the oral teachings of the apostles were the same as their written teaching. Paul referred to the fact that teaching was given by word or letter (2 Thess. 2:2 NKJV). As memory of the oral teaching of the inspired apostles began to fade, the written words of the inspired apostles and prophets were increasingly circulated. God never left his people without the teaching and authority of the inspired apostles. It was primarily in oral form in the beginning, but gradually it came to be available in written form and that is the only reliable form in which we have it today.

My wife, Beverly, sometimes asks me to buy eggs, bacon and orange juice when I'm planning to go to town. However, since she knows I'm forgetful, when I walk out the door, she often hands me a slip of paper with the items written down, "eggs, bacon and orange juice." The fact that she told me orally what she wanted before writing it down, doesn't imply any conflict nor that I should take her written instructions less seriously. The fact that the apostles' teaching existed first orally before being written down and becoming readily available in that form should in no way make us take their written teaching as being less authoritative. It was the same teaching!

God has protected his word. Jesus said. "Heaven and earth shall pass away but my words will not pass away" (Matthew

24:35). If God has gone through so much effort to put us on this planet and send his Son to die for us, would he allow the words that he wanted us to have to be corrupted and/or lost?

2. Trusting Subjective Feelings As Revelation

A young woman whose pastor wanted to buy a building owned by brethren in Upper Manhattan pulled me aside and told me, "the Lord has told me that Pastor Oliveiri will own this whole city block." She was obviously very sincere and wanted me to accept God's will that she felt had been revealed to her.

A brother in the Domini- *"A brother in the Dominican* can Republic dreamed that *Republic dreamed that he* he would marry one of the *would marry one of the* sisters in his congregation. *sisters in his congregation."* He sincerely believed it to be a revelation from God and began to pursue the matter with the sister who felt uncomfortable with his advances.

"You are rejecting God's will for us," the brother told the sister.

Thankfully, the brethren accepted the fact that the dream did not reveal God's will and came to the sister's aid.

A single brother spent the whole night in prayer asking God to help him find a spouse. The next day he was introduced to a young Christian woman and the brother was convinced that she was God's answer to his prayers. However, even though the young woman showed various signs of immaturity, friends had great difficulty in persuading the young man to stop pursuing her because he was sincerely convinced that the young woman was God's answer to his prayers. Thankfully, all involved have matured, but for a period of time, trust in a subjective source of revelation, a chance encounter after a night of prayer, almost resulted in spiritual mistake.

As Postmodernism has deemphasized the importance of the written word, there has been a corresponding emphasis on trust in subjective feeling. Anthropologist T.M. Luhrman quotes a survey in her book, *When God Talks Back*, that "26% of all Americans say they have been given a direct revelation by God."[30] Gary Gilley, in his excellent book *Is That You Lord?*,[31] which I highly recommend, refers to a number of popular Evangelical leaders such as Henry Blackaby, Wayne Grudem and Jack Deere who promote the concept of God's leading apart from the word.

People from relatively conservative congregations speak of God putting something "on their heart" or of God leading them through life's experiences. Though some of these expressions could be taken biblically if they referred to being led by the influence of word, context often makes it doubtful that they have God's written word in mind, but rather subjective feelings. A popular preacher gave a sermon in which he constantly repeated the phrase, "Get in touch with your feelings!" The primary emphasis in the Bible is to get in touch with God on the basis of his word. However, feelings, hunches, impulses, "leadings," promptings, "providential nudges," inner voices, "open doors" are replacing the word of God as the primary source of revelation in the minds of many. Udo W. Middleton lamented, "Our age has largely replaced real discussions of theological, philosophical and cultural content with 'personal' testimony, anecdotal experience and private views."[32]

The Bible teaches that first century revelation given to the apostles is "all truth" (John 16:13), was given once for all and not in little pieces to be revealed throughout human history

(Jude 3), given exclusively through Christ (Heb. 1:1,2), accompanied by apostolic miracles (Hebrews 2:1-4) and that no man has a right to add to it or take away from it under threat of divine judgment (Rev. 22:18, 19). Gary Gilley points out that when Paul wrote his last letter to Timothy, "he did not encourage Timothy to focus on new revelations, impressions, feelings on hunches, Rather he continually turned him to the Word of God and the doctrines contained therein" (2 Tim. 2:2-14, 15; 3:15-17; 4:2-4).[33]

While many give lip service to the sufficiency of the scriptures, their references to knowing God's will through perceived answers to prayers, "providential nudges," hunches and the like reveal that they aren't quite satisfied with them. "While never denying the authority of Scripture as such, many from people in the pew to key leaders, regularly point to mystical experiences as the basis of much of what they do and believe."[34] O. Palmer Robinson says, "If you declare a need for both (scripture and mystical leadings), you have implied the insufficiency of the one."[35]

The lack of confidence in the sufficiency of the scriptures as God's only revelation is one of the curses of the Postmodern influence. It leads people away from Christ, his revelation and his salvation.

3. Uncertain Standard of Right and Wrong

The further one strays from confidence in God's absolute standard of right and wrong, the more difficulty he will have in establishing any system of morals or ethics. The final outcome of the departure from an absolute moral pattern will be the loss of civilization and a downward spiral into the law of the jungle. Romans 1:18ff describes what happens to a culture that is rejecting God. After describing idolatry and sexual perversion, Paul continues in verses 28 through 31 by describing the rotten attitudes that accompany the distancing of a society from God.

> 28   And just as they did not see fit to acknowledge God any longer, God gave them over to a depraved mind, to do those things which are not proper,
>
> 29   being filled with all unrighteousness, wickedness, greed, evil; full of envy, murder, strife, deceit, malice; they are gossips,
>
> 30   slanderers, haters of God, insolent, arrogant, boastful, inventors of evil, disobedient to parents,
>
> 31   without understanding, untrustworthy, unloving, unmerciful;

The French philosophers who trashed the concept that any reality can come from words ("metanarratives") have been rightly attacked on this very point. An anonymous author of an article on Jean-François Lyotard expressed it this way with his philosophical language, "But universals are impermissible in a world that has lost faith in metanarratives, and so it would seem that ethics is impossible."[36] Yes indeed! To question the authority of words from God undermines the system of ethics that has served as the basis for the best aspects of Western Culture. How can you say that anything is wrong without an objective standard? Modernists who deny the existence of God have the same problem. Science without God is as helpless to promote good behavior as Postmodern philosophers.

Some try to wiggle out of this difficulty by stating that whatever hurts other people is wrong. But if Postmodern presuppositions and atheism are correct, determining which actions hurt and which help is a matter of subjective opinion. Hitler thought that he was helping society by liquidating the mentally feeble and those of "undesirable" races. Mao and Pol Pot thought they were cleansing their countries of undesirables to prepare the rest for Utopian Communism. If authoritative words and standards are rejected, there is no objective criterion to condemn their atrocities. You might have one opinion about what hurts others and they have another. Whoever has the most guns wins the argument!

Though many don't realize the consequences of their reasoning, religious people who begin to question the authority or understandability of the Bible will sooner or later begin to head down the same road towards spiritual anarchy. Though the fact that they have been taught scriptural principles may restrain them somewhat during their lifetimes, their children and grandchildren will take their questioning of **"...Their reasoning will lead us to much more than a little guitar to go with the singing! "** God's authority to its logical extreme and approve and practice things their parents could never have imagined. Though they are correct when condemning those who are carnal and merciless when analyzing the scriptures to find God's authority, they are dangerously wrong when questioning the very existence of understandable divine authority in the scriptures.

Among known churches of Christ, few who complain about requiring Biblical authority to authorize spiritual practices seem to consider the logical outcome of discarding that scriptural approach. Though certainly they won't go as far nor as fast towards spiritual anarchy as French philosophers, their questioning of man's ability to respond to objective authority carries more serious consequences than they seem to realize. They would like to get rid of the concept of a Biblical pattern so that they can have a little instrumental music or defend their favorite denominational machinery, but do not consider the fact that their reasoning will lead us to much more than a little guitar to go with the singing! If there's no Biblical pattern regarding church organization and worship, the development of the Roman Catholic hierarchy was no big deal. We could all have a universal pope, a college of cardinals, regional bishops who control dioceses, etc. We could worship with candles, incense, holy water, etc. and that would be fine. If there is no real Biblical pattern, or if it's practically indecipherable, what's wrong with all of that? Only a very few who have been influenced by the Restoration Movement and who rebel against the concept of a Biblical pattern seem to realize that that's where their thinking will lead.

I had a blog exchange about instrumental music with the editor of a progressive publication among brethren and asked him if his reasoning wouldn't justify laser lights and fog machines in worship to God. He responded by comparing laser shows and fog machines to Powerpoint presentations! I decided to take it a step further and asked him at what point elements in Catholic worship such as holy water, rosaries, candles, etc. should have been opposed by Christians in the centuries after Christ. He responded that since he wasn't a Catholic, such elements wouldn't mean much to him, but it was clear that he wouldn't say that the additions of such elements into worship would be wrong! To have said they were would have been inconsistent with what he was saying to justify instrumental music in worship and he knew it.

When pressed about the consequences of their rejection of a Biblical pattern, I've noticed that many of my more progressive brethren will state that they *prefer* practices that we see from Bible examples but can't bring themselves to state that such practices are the only ones authorized. I'll give three examples.

(1) "Congregational organization" - A friend I made on the Internet wrote that we shouldn't insist so strongly on limiting ourselves to following Bible examples regarding church organization because that type of issue isn't the essence of the gospel of Christ. "A focus on love and the death and resurrection of Christ are the heart of the gospel," he pointed out, "not church organization."

I responded that though church organization, of course, isn't as weighty as love, mercy and faith, we shouldn't consider it completely unimportant. According to many historians the first sign of the apostasy that eventually resulted in the development of the Roman church was a simple change in that "unimportant" area of congregational organization, the acceptance of

> *"I asked if it would be acceptable then for churches to enter into all kinds of businesses: Church of Christ banks, Church of Christ real estate companies, etc."*

a presiding bishop. I then asked him whether early congregations should have been concerned about having only one bishop in a congregation along with regional bishops and archbishops. When pressured a bit he finally stated that he *preferred* that there be a plurality of bishops in each congregation.

(2) How congregations raise funds - Another friend stated that we shouldn't take 1 Corinthians 16:1-4 as an exclusive pattern regarding church fund raising. He believed, for example, that young people could raise funds for the church by washing cars.

I asked if it would be acceptable then for churches to enter into all kinds of businesses: Church of Christ banks, Church of Christ real estate companies, etc. He responded that he *preferred* that congregations generally raise needed money by voluntary offerings of the members.

(3) The use of watermelon in the Lord's Supper - When a progressive brother was pressed as to whether his reasoning wouldn't permit using watermelon as a third emblem in the Lord's table, he responded, "I *personally* wouldn't do this, just as I *personally* would not have added the four cups of wine to the Passover feast. But that is just my own preference in the matter."[37] (Emphasis his)

So our brother would *prefer* not to have watermelon in the Lord's Supper, but that's just a personal *preference*. (Incidentally, his reasoning is wrong in comparing watermelon in the Lord's Supper to four cups of wine at the Passover. God did not specify what to drink at the Passover meal, thus giving the Jews liberty to choose. He did specify bread as the food at the Lord's Supper and therefore watermelon would be a presumptuous addition.)

Personal preference is not a sufficient standard. It would have not been effective in restraining the development of Romanism—"We prefer not to have regional bishops or a pope. We prefer not to venerate images or sprinkle babies." Personal preference is not adequate to restrain the human tendency to apostatize from God today. However, personal preference is all that those influenced by Postmodernism have since they reject the concept of a Biblical pattern.

Man must have a divine standard. He was designed to function well only with that standard. The same thing is true of congregations that follow Christ. The further we are from God's perfect standard, the more we suffer collectively and individually. Even imperfect standards like Islam and Eastern Religions are better than none at all, though how much they help their respective cultures will depend on how close they are to God's ideal standard. This type of thinking is complete heresy to Postmodernists (if there were such thing as heresy in their minds, and in this case there probably is), but it is truth.

Questions for thought

1. Why do you think God chose words as a vehicle for the revelation of his truth?

2. Why does man want to get away from the concept of God's written authority? What abuses might have helped promote the desire to get away from it?

3. Why is it important to understand that our thoughts and impulses are not direct revelations from God?

4. Can our thoughts and impulses come from God in an indirect way, even though they are not direct revelations from him? How does that happen?

5. Why are those who are trying to distance themselves from the concept of God's written authority so unwilling to face the consequences of their approach?

6. Why is it so important to distinguish between which practices might involve personal preference and which involve following God's will. What would be some practices you would put in the area of personal preference? What practices would belong in the area of following God's will?

Thoughts for prayer: Thankfulness for "wonderful words of life," wisdom in dealing with Postmodern influences, prayer for our Western countries and cultures as they are sliding away from God; for churches and families that are increasingly affected by Postmodernism.

Chapter 6

Jesus, A Man of Conviction

An Exaggerated and Fictitious Comparison

"Johnny Regulations" sees Christianity primarily as a matter of following rules. His favorite verses are 2 John 9; John 14:15; 1 John 2:3 and others that give emphasis to punishment. He likes to talk about hell, Nadab and Abihu and apostasy. He reads a lot in the Bible but not so much to edify himself as to find texts he can use to combat those with whom he disagrees.

Johnny gets very uncomfortable when others begin to talk about God's mercy, patience, grace, love and similar concepts. He wonders if they might be liberal and soft on sin. He's quick to remind others that God is a consuming fire.

Johnny is only comfortable with people of his party. He often asks suspiciously about others, "Is he with us or with them?"

If he thinks that some brother is "with them," he begins to eye him suspiciously and wonders how he might be able to expose him.

He doesn't spend much time visiting those who are sick or in serving others. It's not that Johnny is a completely bad person, but serving others isn't a big priority in his life because in his mind, Christianity is primarily a matter of following rules that he has cataloged in his mind from the New Testament, much like many Jews came to see serving God as a matter of following 613 regulations that they extracted from the Old Testament.[38]

"Bobby Hugs" sees Christianity primarily as a means of showing affection. He constantly hugs others and walks around with a silly grin on his face. "God is love," quotes Bobby and his favorite verses are 1 John 3:18, 1 Corinthians 13 and others that emphasize love.

Bobby gets nervous if you start to talk about apostasy and error. "Don't talk about doctrine. Talk about Jesus!" he says, forgetting the fact that the word "doctrine" simply means "teaching" and that it is impossible to talk about Jesus without talking about his teaching!

Bobby doesn't educate himself about apostasy and errors among his known brethren. "There's got to be unity," he says and therefore doesn't want to say that anyone is wrong about anything. "That's being judgmental," says Bobby.

They've both missed it! Johnny accuses Bobby of being a weak-kneed, pussyfooted compromiser and he's right. Bobby dismisses Johnny as being a humorless and cold reactionary and he's right. Both are right in seeing the other's defects, but wrong in only emphasizing one aspect of Christ's character. Neither imitates the Master.

Jesus, a Man of Conviction

Anyone who went to the temple to worship a few days before the Passover, probably in A.D. 27, would have had any quiet thoughts interrupted by pure pandemonium as he passed by the area where money was changed and animals were sold for sacrifices. The first sound to have invaded his sensitivities would have been the crashing of tables accompanied by the sound of coins being scattered and rolling around on the pavement, followed by the alarmed bellowing of cattle and bleating of sheep. A closer look would have seen an imposing figure dressed in country garb with a small whip in his hand driving the raucous animals as their handlers either cowered in the corner or ran for cover. The man with a small scourge of cords, would have been shouting to those huddled by the cages of doves the Aramaic equivalent of, "get this stuff out of here!"

The cleansing of the temple hurts the postmodern sensitivities of those who would prefer to see Jesus of Nazareth as a kind of Caspar Milquetoast figure who never raised his voice. E.P. Sanders says that the incident was possibly "a singular flash of anger" and discounts the possibility that it was an effective part of Jesus' mission.[39] In writing about the event he complained, "A real reformer, should have more of a programme of reform than Jesus seems to have had."[40] There's no doubt that if there were such a thing as a "ministerial association" in Jerusalem, that Jesus would have been cast out of it for behavior unbecoming to the clergy! However, the actions of Jesus were completely compatible with the fact that he was a man of conviction. He loved his heavenly Father and despised any action of men that distracted from the will of the Father and from his holiness and purity. Polluting what should have been a place of prayer with common commerce was a gross violation of all that he stood for and divine indignation was the only logical response, both at the beginning and the end of his ministry.

The convictions of Jesus and his authoritative style of teaching separated him instantly from the scribes and other religious teachers of the day and put him at odds with them. Matthew mentions that at the end of the Sermon on the Mount, "the crowds were amazed at His teaching; for He was teaching them as one having authority, and not as their scribes."[41]

Paul Earnhart describes the teaching style of the scribes.

> The largely mindless scribes, no real students of the law itself and with hardly an original thought, spent their days studying and collating what ancient influential rabbis had said about the law. They suspended their arguments from endless strings of rabbinic quotations and fanciful interpretations.[42]

In contrast, Jesus' teaching "resounded with the deep ring of confident truth.... It is inevitable that the voice of God will sound like God." Earnhart also emphasized the fact that the words of Jesus came from a profound love and concern for those who heard him as opposed to the scribes' desire to manipulate words for their own advantage.

A Man of Conviction
in Dealing with the Sadducees and Pharisees

The convictions of Jesus can also be seen in his disdain for the religious compromisers of his day, the Sadducees. The origin of the Sadducees can be traced to political maneuvering of the Jews, just after the time of the Maccabees.[43] Many in this exclusive party were descendants of that revered family and became the sect of the high priests that controlled Jewish government. From their position of wealth and power, the Sadducees fought to maintain their privileged status, accepting many Greek ideas but compromising when necessary with their more nationalistic and popular antagonists, the Pharisees.

Some Jewish compromisers like the Sadducees dressed like the Greeks, gave Greek names to their children, exercised nude in the gymnasiums and a few even surgically reversed their circumcisions, much to the chagrin of more conservative Jews.[44] As far as their attitude towards scripture, the Sadducees claimed to respect them, and yet were quick to allegorize them, saying that they had a hidden and unknown meaning, especially when they contradicted the prevalent Greek philosophy. Luke points out that like the Greeks, they did not believe in angels nor in the resurrection (Acts 23:8). Though Philo of Alexandria was not a Sadducee, his dismissal of those who would not take the scriptures allegorically as "sophists of literalness"[45] would have probably reflected their view.

The Sadducees, unlike the Pharisees who opposed Jesus from the very beginning, seemed to become alarmed about Jesus primarily during the latter stages of his life. After the resurrection of Lazarus, the High Priest decided something had to be done, so he organized a meeting with their enemies the Pharisees. There was a consensus about the problem, "If we let Him go on like this, all men will believe in Him, and the Romans will come and take away both our place and our nation" (John 11:48). The wily high priest of the old ruling class, Caiphas retorted, unknowingly inspired by the Spirit, "You know nothing at all, nor do you take into account that it is expedient for you that one man die for the people, and that the whole nation not perish" (John 11:49b, 50).

The primary clash of Jesus with the Sadducees occurred just before his death and is recorded in all three of the synoptic gospels (Matt. 22:23-33; Mark 12:18-27 and Luke 20:27-40). Apparently, the Sadducees loved to make fun of their opponents by showing how their beliefs led to ridiculous conclusions.[46] They thought they would make Jesus look absurd in his teaching about the resurrection by asking him about a woman with seven husbands and asking which one would be hers in the resurrection.

Jesus' answer was twofold: (1) Marriage will not be a relationship after the resurrection and (2) the Sadducees were inconsistent in rejecting the idea of life after death when Jehovah plainly stated that he was God of the living Abraham, Isaac and Jacob hundreds of years after their deaths (Exodus 3:6; 15,16).

Notice that Jesus did not dismiss the error of the Sadducees as a simple mistake of sincere people and that since God is merciful and since we should emphasize grace, such would best be ignored. Rather, as a man of conviction, he met the error head on, using simple logic through words to expose it. Jesus was no Postmodernist!

"...He met the error head on, using simple logic through words to expose it. Jesus was no Postmodernist!"

Jesus had more clashes with the Pharisees than with the Sadducees, probably not because the error of the latter was any less dangerous than the Pharisees, but rather because the Pharisees were more popular with the masses (since they were nationalistic) and opposed Jesus earlier in his preaching ministry.

The Pharisees can be traced to the Hasidim of the Second Century before Christ, pious men who resisted the growing Greek influences among the leading class that eventually became the Sadducees.[47] Though Pharisaism has already been discussed in chapter 3, the point to be made here about them is the fact that Jesus' convictions would not allow him to ignore its excesses. He confronted them directly, especially in chapters like Matthew 23, perhaps hoping to open the eyes of some Pharisees, but probably even more, to warn those who might sympathize with their shallow approach to serving God.

Questions for thought

1. Have you ever known anyone like "Johnny Regulations" or "Bobby Hugs." Why is it so easy to get into one of those two molds and miss the essence of what it means to be like Christ?

2. How do you think Jesus' cleansing of the temple would be reported in most newspapers today or on the television news? How do you think most "clergy" would see such an action?

3. Should we imitate Jesus' actions and literally go into bingo halls and church bazaars turning over tables? Why or why not? What might be some differences between Jesus' situation and ours? If we shouldn't literally go into such places and turn over tables, what are some ways we can try to combat the materialism and worldliness in churches?

4. How can we teach "with authority" without coming across as being arrogant or self righteous?

5. Does it seem that Jesus criticized the Pharisees more than the Sadducees? Why might that have been the case?

Thoughts for prayer: The need to avoid the extremes of those like "Bobby Hugs" and "Johnny Regulations;" help in knowing how to best encourage such people to be more like Christ; wisdom to know when to toss out the moneychangers and when to correct gently.

Chapter 7

Jesus, The Ideal Combination of Conviction and Mercy, Part 2, Mercy

Jesus, A Man of Mercy

Though Jesus as a man of conviction was a fierce warrior in fighting the errors of the Pharisees, Sadducees and other proud members of the religious establishment, he was also "gentle and humble in heart" (Matthew 11:29). He would not "break a bruised reed" (Is. 42:3; Matt. 12:20, ESV).

Perhaps this aspect of the Son of God is best seen in his attitude towards the despised and downtrodden. The main characters in his stories are not heroic generals, admired athletes or noted scholars, but rather farmers, fishermen, housekeepers, merchants and perhaps more surprising than anyone else, the despised Samaritans!

The Samaritans were historical enemies of the Jews, resisting their resettlement in Jerusalem (Ezra 4:2; Nehemiah 4:7ff) and often harassing Jews traveling between Galilee and Jerusalem. When Jewish leaders ridiculed Jesus as a Samaritan possessed by a demon (John 8:48), they were obviously using a common form of vilification. In choosing Samaritans to be heroes of his stories, particularly the healing of the ten lepers and the good Samaritan (Luke 17:11-19; 10:29-37), Jesus showed no desire to please his Jewish audience but rather to shake them. When considering the depth of hatred between the Samaritans and Jews, it isn't hard to imagine the grimaces and eye-rolling when Jesus portrayed the Samaritans in such a positive light. The positive depiction of the Samaritans to Jewish audiences would be like using members of the Taliban as good role models for Americans.

The attitude of Jesus towards Samaritans reveals his unfathomable mercy. Their doctrine was a confused jumble of Mosaic law mixed with various pagan elements and their attitude towards God's people, the Jews, was often hostile (Luke 9:53). Jesus didn't overlook their errors, gently reminding the Samaritan woman in John 4 that they worshipped what they didn't know and that salvation is of the Jews (vs. 22). However, his portrayal of them is almost entirely positive, especially when contrasted with his approach to the Pharisees who were much more doctrinally correct.

The great mercy of Jesus is also seen in his eating companions and friends (Matt. 9:9-12; Mark 2:16, 17; Luke 15:1, 2). He ate with tax collectors and sinners. A sinful woman was confident enough to approach him in the house of Simon the Pharisee and anoint his feet with costly perfume (Luke 7:36ff). This association earned him the sarcastic rebuke of his Pharisee friends, but left an indelible record to his profound grace. Jesus did not condone their sinful ways when associating with them, but by doing so showed them his great love and therefore was able to call them to repentance on the basis of that love (Mark 2:17).

The merciful desire of Jesus to open his life and heart to the dregs of society is seldom reproduced, especially in the United States. It is easy to bask in the material blessings that have come from the zealous work ethic that our forefathers learned from the influence of the Bible. From our sanitized suburbs it is common to watch the television news about mayhem and murder in the housing projects downtown and grumble about those who won't learn personal responsibility to get an education and a job. It is also easy to see scenes of poverty and war in other parts of the world and point out with justification that such suffering comes in increasing measure the further away a culture is from God. However, it is difficult to seek ways to show the mercy of Jesus and actually do something concrete to help such people.

The Perfect Mixture of Conviction and Mercy - Jesus with the Apostles

To paraphrase a godly preacher of the past century from Eastern Kentucky, Henry Ficklin, the twelve apostles must have been Jesus' "dearest problems." Time and time again they revealed their immaturity and lack of faith. A few examples:

• Arguing over who was the greatest (Luke 9:46)

• Asking for fire to come down and destroy a Samaritan village (Luke 9:54)

• Showing inability to cast out a demon in a young boy (Luke 9:40).

• Doubting that they would have enough food after Jesus fed the 5000 (Matthew 16:9)

• Chasing away children who wanted to see Jesus (Luke 18:15)

• Wanting to sit on his right and left hand in the kingdom (Mark 10:37)

• Peter's unbelief when slipping beneath the waves (Matt. 14:30)

• Peter's "foot in the mouth" when he proposed to make three tabernacles on the mount of transfiguration (Luke 9:33)

• Peter's rebuke of Jesus for saying that he would suffer and die in Jerusalem (Mark 8:32)

• Fleeing when he was arrested (Matt. 26:56)

• Peter's denial (Matt. 26:69ff)

• Disbelieving the women's testimony about Jesus' resurrection (Luke 24:11)

When Jesus said on numerous occasions, "O you of little faith," it is not hard to imagine him putting his face in his hands in frustration. Certainly many of those hours of prayer to his Heavenly Father must have been filled with anguished pleas for those weak men the Father had given him.

And yet, the time Jesus spent with his apostles wasn't spent in denunciation but in patient teaching. Jesus didn't wash his hands of the apostles, dismissing them as hopeless, but rather he praised them as much as possible.

• "Truly I say to you, that you who have followed Me, in the regeneration when the Son of Man will sit on His glorious throne, you also shall sit upon twelve thrones, judging the twelve tribes of Israel" (Matt. 19:28).

• When asked if he and the other disciples would join the multitudes who were abandoning Jesus, Simon Peter answered Him, "Lord, to whom shall we go? You have words of eternal life. We have believed and have come to know that You are the Holy One of God." Jesus answered him, "Did I Myself not choose you, the twelve...?" (John 6:68-70)

John 17

Perhaps the mercy of Jesus towards the apostles can be seen in John 17 more than any other passage in the New Testament. There the Holy Spirit gives us a glimpse into the communication between God the Son and God the Father and much of it has to do with those twelve stumbling men that we call the apostles. After praying for personal strength in verses 1-5, Jesus pours out his heart to the Father regarding the twelve. Verse 6 is especially astounding, "I have manifested Your name to the men whom You gave Me out of the world; they were Yours and You gave them to Me, and they have kept Your word."

The last phrase, "They have kept Your word," is attention grabbing because it refers to men who were guilty of all those misconceptions and pride mentioned several paragraphs earlier. How could Jesus say of such weak men, "They have kept Your word?"

Perhaps the best explanation is to understand that Jesus must have looked at his apostles much as we look at our children. We warn them of the unpleasant consequences of their immaturity and disobedience—"As long as you live under this roof, you're going to have to obey better than that!" And yet, it would rightly take acts of outright rebellion for us to actually kick teenagers out of the family and onto the street. If you asked me if my daughters were obedient when in our home, I might think of occasions where they conveniently "didn't hear me" or after many threats, finally cleaned the kitchen in slow motion. However, I could answer honestly that yes they were obedient, taking into consideration that generally they did want to obey even though they "had their moments." Certainly that was the only way Jesus could say of the apostles, "they have kept your word." Though grieved on occasions at their lack of maturity, he looked upon them with mercy, praising them to his Father. His life was the perfect combination of conviction and mercy!

The Letters to the Seven Churches of Asia

"All local churches in the first century taught and practiced the same thing."

That type of declaration isn't uncommon in tracts and Bible studies about the church from the 1960's and earlier. The only problem is that it wasn't so. Congregations in the first century attained different levels of growth and understanding and dealt with spiritual challenges of those days with different levels of effectiveness. Perhaps no portion of the scripture illustrates the fallacy of unanimity of churches better than the letters to the seven churches of Asia in Revelation 2 and 3.

Of the seven churches of Asia, two (Sardis and Laodicea) were in critical condition and were in imminent danger of losing their candlesticks; two (Smyrna and Philadelphia) were praised and received no correction and the other three had a mixture of good qualities and serious problems.

As would be expected, the response of Jesus to these different churches reflects a mixture of stern warnings and gentle mercy.

• "I am coming to you and will remove your lamp stand out of its place– unless you repent" (2:5).

• "Behold, I will throw her on a bed of sickness, and those who commit adultery with her into great tribulation, unless they repent of her deeds" (2:22).

• "To him who overcomes... I will give the morning star" (2:26, 28).

• "He who overcomes will thus be clothed in white garments; and I will not erase his name from the book of life, and I will confess his name before My Father and before His angels" (3:5).

• "So because you are lukewarm, and neither hot nor cold, I will spit you out of My mouth" (3:16).

Jesus Christ was the perfect combination of conviction and mercy in dealing with the seven churches of Asia.

Paul's Combination of Conviction and Mercy

As one of the most dedicated followers of Christ, the apostle Paul reflected his master's astounding combination of conviction and mercy.

He heaped praise on the Corinthians on occasions, "that in everything you were enriched in Him, in all speech and all knowledge, even as the testimony concerning Christ was confirmed in you" (1 Cor. 1:5,6). Later he was scathing in his denunciations and even sarcastic.

• "For you, being so wise, tolerate the foolish gladly" (2 Cor. 11:19).

• "I say in advance to those who have sinned in the past and to all the rest as well, that if I come again I will not spare anyone" (2 Cor. 13:2).

To the Thessalonians, Paul could be "gentle among you, as a nursing mother tenderly cares for her own children" (1 Thess. 2:7), but he could also exhort them to "keep away from every brother who leads an unruly life and not according to the tradition which you received from us" (2 Thess. 3:6).

This combination of conviction and mercy was essential to imitating Christ and helping the Corinthians and Thessalonians see the spiritual danger they were in, but doing so in love.

When to Emphasize Conviction and When Mercy?

Both conviction and mercy were a permanent part of Christ's divine makeup. His dealings with others didn't involve turning one on and the other off. Though one aspect, his conviction, might have been more apparent when he dealt with the Pharisees, that doesn't mean that he had no mercy, nor did the mercy with the apostles mean that he had no convictions. It was a package deal!

Imitators of Jesus will also simultaneously be characterized by conviction and mercy. One quality or the other may be more evident in some circumstances than in the other. Jude acknowledged this in Jude 22, 23 when discussing three types of situations that saints might have to deal with. "And have mercy on some, who are doubting; save others, snatching them out of the fire; and on some have mercy with fear, hating even the garment polluted by the flesh."

Notice the three categories in Jude 22,23: (1) The doubting need to be treated with mercy, (2) those in immediate spiritual danger need to be "snatched from the fire" and (3) those with contaminating sin need to be treated with a mixture of mercy and fear. It's not that those in immediate spiritual danger need no mercy, but rather that mercy may not be the most noticeable characteristic when snatching someone from the fire.

It is sometimes difficult on occasions to know when to "be gentle as a nursing mother" and when to "not spare anyone." Knowing which spiritual condition requires which approach is one of the biggest challenges we have when striving to imitate Christ in helping others. Years of studying his approach and years of practice and prayer help in properly combining conviction and mercy. Generally speaking, Jesus emphasized mercy more with those who were babes, were striving to grow and make a genuine effort to seek the Father. His strong convictions were more evident when dealing with those who were hypocrites, rebellious, promoting their false teaching and should have known better.

May God help his people to develop that amazing combination of conviction and mercy that characterized his Son, Jesus Christ, so that we can better reflect his glory and love in our lives!

Questions for thought

1. Why do you think Jesus chose the Samaritans as positive models in several of his parables and stories? Was he trying to say that their errors didn't matter? What "down and out" groups of people might he use if trying to make the same point today? Would he be criticized for looking at the positive aspects of such groups?

2. How can we build bridges to help those who are spiritually down and out and not be standoffish towards them without allowing ourselves to be affected by their errors? (These are tough questions but important to consider!)

3. Did the apostles keep God's word? Can God say the same thing about us even though we, like them, are sometimes imperfect in our understanding and growth? Does this console you? Does this fact give us an excuse to sin or to see sin as "not so bad"?

4. Does the fact that a congregation has some error in it mean that it is automatically not a church of Christ? What examples, besides those of the seven churches of Asia, can be given to illustrate this point? Does this fact mean that correction of the error should be any less urgent?

5. How does Jude 22, 23 show that different types of spiritual diseases require different types of approaches for spiritual healing? Why do we often want to use a "one size fits all" approach when trying to help friends with spiritual problems? Why is this harmful?

Thoughts for prayer: To be more like Jesus and develop that remarkable combination of conviction and mercy; wisdom to know how to reach out more effectively to modern day Samaritans, tax collectors and sinners; thanksgiving for God's mercy and patience with us as we've gone through different stages of halting spiritual growth.

Chapter 8

Who's the Enemy? Part 1

E nglish novelist Joseph Conrad said, "You shall judge a man by his foes as well as his friends."[48] Those who have no enemies are bland and convictionless with no love or passion. All the prophets of the Old Testament were fervently against something, in particular whatever was pulling God's people away from him. Those who prophesied around the time of the exile like Jeremiah and Ezekiel abhorred idolatry. Later prophets like Haggai and Malachi despised the apathy that was beginning to characterize the Jewish nation.

Jesus constantly battled the spiritual establishment of his day and he warned his disciples that the same must be true of them if they were going to follow him. "Woe to you when all men speak well of you" (Luke 6:26). He came not to bring peace but a sword (Matt. 10:34). Those who have convictions will have enemies, even as they work to balance their convictions with mercy.

Different Enemies Threaten at Different Times

Parents worry about childhood diseases like measles, mumps and chicken pox in their children. Older adults worry more about heart disease, prostate cancer, breast cancer, Alzheimer's, etc.

Joshua warned the Israelites about Egyptian gods (Joshua 24:14). Though Egypt's influence would always endanger God's people, after they moved into the land of promise, Canaanite and Mesopotamian gods began to become more of a focus as the enemy (Judges 2:12). After the exile, idolatry wasn't as obvious as an enemy as were apathy and discouragement (Haggai, Zachariah). By the time Jesus arrived, the spiritual pride of the Sadducees and Pharisees threatened the Jews. Paul's early letters reveal a strong concern about Judaizing teachers, while his later epistles seem to reflect his concern over early Gnosticism. The persecution of evil worldly powers was the big enemy in the book of Revelation.

None of the enemies mentioned above ever ceased completely to be dangerous, but the level of danger each one represented waxed and waned throughout the history of God's people. Therefore, the level of attention they received from God's prophets also varied. Egyptian gods could still have been a danger in the post exilic period, but they weren't the focus of the prophets of that period.

Not only do different enemies threaten more or less at different stages of history, but also at different stages of our lives. Paul warned about youthful lusts in 2 Timothy 2:22, acknowledging that some are stronger when hormones are more active. The different exhortations given to different groups of Christians in Titus 2 indicate that some challenges are greater at different stages in life. Paul specifies that older men be sound in love and patience, perhaps addressing the grouchy old men syndrome. Older women are told to not be given to much wine. Older women today may have more of a temptation than others to become dependent on pain pills (perhaps an equivalent of wine), and thus Paul addresses that specific enemy in exhorting them. Younger men are told to be careful to have sound speech that cannot be condemned.

Even today, that group is probably more tempted to repeat the crude expressions of their worldly peers.

Different Perspectives on Today's Greatest Enemy

What is the biggest enemy facing disciples of the Lord today? The answer will probably depend on the age of the person you ask. Christians influenced by more conservative elements of the Stone-Campbell restoration movement, who are over forty years of age and who have been influenced by religious rationalism will give answers like these:

• **Denominationalism** - Fear that compromise with mainstream Protestant groups and Evangelical thought and practices will lead to acceptance of errors of those groups and the loss of respect for truths that Protestantism traditionally rejects.

• **Liberalism** - Loose attitudes towards biblical authority, especially regarding worship practices and organization in local churches.

• **Institutionalism** - This was the big battle of the 1950's and 1960's.

Disciples under 40 years of age will probably be inclined to give answers like the following:

• **Traditionalism** - Doing things because we've always done them, not because of loving God.

• **Pharisaism** - Overemphasizing the externals and underemphasizing the heart.

• **Lack of emphasis on God's grace** - Trusting in works without sufficiently considering God's grace.

Sometimes in giving their answers both groups probably overlook several of the greatest enemies: worldliness, selfishness and a lack of love. Understanding the perspectives of both groups will help us imitate Jesus in emphasizing both convictions and mercy.

Fighting Denominations

Early "restorers" fought mainstream denominations for being divisive and for taking the focus off of Christ for guidance and putting it on their human creeds, institutions and networks. Alexander Campbell fought the established religious denominations in his early years, though he seemed to make accommodations with them later in his life. Raccoon John Smith clashed with Baptists, Presbyterians, Methodists and others throughout Eastern Kentucky as he went about establishing congregations. Most mainstream denominations promoted Calvinism which was anathema especially to Barton W. Stone and Raccoon John Smith who had studied their way out of it. Calvinists, of course, rejected the doctrine of baptism for the remission of sins, which became one of the doctrines that most distinguished those influenced by Stone and Campbell from mainstream Protestants.

Some second and third generation preachers in the Restoration Movement were probably even more aggressive in taking on denominations. We laugh today at the title of an old publication that began in 1837, *Heretic Detector*, edited by an early disciple influenced by Campbell, Arthur Crihfield. His attitude towards traditional Protestant teaching can easily be surmised.

While doing research on our family's history, I found that a preacher named Rees Jones who had been influenced by Barton Stone was the first to preach to my ancestors in 1847 in Hall's Valley near Trion, Georgia. Then I found an article written about Jones by J.D. Floyd in the *Gospel Advocate* in 1911. Floyd said that Rees Jones "had a warlike style of preaching" because of the persecution at hands of denominations.[49] Though that type of description would probably fit many preachers from the Nineteenth Century and first half of the Twentieth Centuries, I wonder how many today could be described that way?

Gentlemanly David Lipscomb appreciated rough-hewn J.D. Tant's unflagging determination, but at the same time must have cringed often at his crude and merciless condemnations of denominational preachers. After hearing that Tant's debate with John T. Oakley in 1900 was filled with "personalities and coarseness," he refused to report about it in the *Gospel Advocate* and some of Tant's supporters took that as a slight. Tant, however, wasn't offended but explained, "no man can kill a polecat without smelling bad."[50]

> *"The view that mainstream denominations were among the greatest enemies to the cause of Christ continued well into the twentieth century."*

The view that mainstream denominations were among the greatest enemies to the cause of Christ continued well into the twentieth century. Notices of debates with holiness groups, Baptists and other Protestant denominations fill the *Gospel Advocate* and other popular journals in the Restoration Movement from the late 1800's through the 1950's. That is certainly not the case now! A high percentage of sermons I heard as a boy in the 1960's, especially at weeklong gospel meetings, was designed to combat Calvinism and other Protestant errors.

Often the bitterness against popular denominations reached extreme levels that concerned those who gave more emphasis to mercy. Foy Short, an evangelist in Southern Africa in the twentieth century, recalled that a college friend from Abilene Christian College in the early 1940's, Ralph Graham, was not only extremely conservative, but also very militant. He had a car with a loudspeaker and on occasions parked it in front of the Methodist or Baptist church with several other preacher boys. They would turn the amplifier up to preach to the Methodists or Baptists inside. The beleaguered churchgoers called the police on several occasions to get relief from the over zealous college boys.[51]

When doing a little research recently, I found that Ralph Graham eventually became a preacher in the Disciples of Christ denomination and wrote an article titled "Why I left the Churches of Christ."[52] I have heard a number of anecdotal stories of men who were harsh and merciless in their condemnations of "liberals" and denominations in their youth, and then in their older age tossed out their convictions and joined them. They never seemed to understand that there can be and even must be a combination of conviction and mercy. Leroy Garrett and Carl Ketcherside are two of the more well known figures in the Stone-Campbell movement who have made the transition from the militant far right to the far left of the spectrum.

In his article about leaving the "Churches of Christ," Graham describes concepts that he had while in his youth that no perceptive disciple should ever have, for example, that men have "restored the church." That is something that only God can do. It is God who saves and who adds people to his body; thus he is the only one who can "restore" it (Acts 2:47). Men don't "restore" the church! Like Hezekiah and Josiah, men can restore principles and practices that have been forgotten through the centuries. but there is a great differences between restoring some forgotten practices and "restoring the church."

Graham also criticized "Churches of Christ" for "presenting the Christian religion in terms of externals." He is right that some have been guilty of that error as he obviously was as a young man. However, he assumed that all others in what he called "Churches of Christ" have had the same harsh, unmerciful approach that he visibly had. He obviously never considered the examples of the many who have combined mercy with their convictions. David Lipscomb would have not been his hero in his days at Abilene Christian College.

The solution in Graham's life would have been to toss out the mercilessness and sectarian concepts without abandoning his convictions and joining a denomination. Those who are ruthless and unloving in their attitudes toward mainstream denominations or liberalism often actually help those systems by driving others into them. Then they often go into them themselves in their later years!

Questions for thought

1. What are some enemies that threatened you more when you were younger than now? What are some enemies that might threaten you more now than when you were younger?

2. Of the "enemies" mentioned, which do you think most threatens God's people today? What are some spiritual enemies not mentioned that you think should concern us?

3. Why do you think religious error seems to be a greater threat in the minds of those disciples who are older than for those who are younger? Why is it hard for younger disciples to see religious error as such a serious danger?

4. Have you ever attended a religious debate? Was it conducted in a gentlemanly way or did it get ugly? What reasons (both good and bad) do you think we can give for the fact that there are few religious debates today? Could they accomplish good if conducted in a loving way?

5. Do you know of anyone who was harsh in condemning others but that eventually lost his convictions and became very tolerant of religious error? Why might this type of transformation take place? Do you know of others who have been overly harsh who made healthy adjustments to become more merciful while still maintaining their convictions?

Thoughts for prayer: To have the same enemies that God has; for strength in dealing with the enemies that most threaten us at various stages of our lives; to have proper attitudes towards those in religious error; to avoid the tendency to swing between being overly harsh and overly tolerant.

Chapter 9

Who's the Enemy? Part 2

Perspectives of Those Who Are Younger

Some younger disciples influenced by the Restoration Movement have a difficult time understanding their parents' aversion to mainstream Evangelicalism. When American culture is overrun with atheism, sexual perversion and the slaughter of innocents, far from being our enemies, Evangelicals are often allies in battling those evils. Most of the best books on apologetics are written by Evangelicals like Paul Copan, William Lane Craig, Ravi Zacharias and Lee Strobel. While their parents often argued with their Baptist friends in high school, teenage disciples today often see serious Baptist and Pentecostal teens as the only friends they have with high moral standards. Though we disagree in many areas with mainstream Evangelicals, it is a fact that they have provided us with great spiritual blessings.

I've noticed the difference in attitudes between older and younger disciples regarding Evangelicalism in their responses to a popular preacher, Francis Chan, mentioned in Chapter four. He is the author of *Crazy Love* that sold 300,000 copies in the first year of publication. His newest book, *Forgotten*

God, has also become popular in Evangelical circles and is circulating among a number of young disciples. Chan is not only dynamic but also extremely sincere in his desire to get away from the comfortable Christianity that is suffocating so many churches with deadening routine and accumulating materialism. He hammers away in his books against common comfort zones and challenges those who claim to be followers of Christ to be led by the Spirit into a self-sacrificing dedication to serve God and others. His enthusiasm is contagious. However, Chan is wrong doctrinally on several important points, writing as if God "illumines" us in mysterious ways.[53] In *Forgotten God* he accepts the possibility that God speaks supernaturally through modern day prophets.[54]

Older disciples who see doctrinal error as one of the big enemies facing God's people are alarmed at such teaching. Younger disciples, who tend to see Pharisaism and traditionalism as more immediate enemies, love Chan's blasts against those evils and seem to overlook the dangers of his subjectivism. Which is the greater enemy, Chan's belief in the possibility of subjective revelations or the comfortable Christianity he assails? The truth is that according to Christ's teaching both are dangers, but those influenced by religious rationalism and younger disciples influenced by Postmodern trends will tend to see Francis Chan in vastly different ways.

"Liberalism"

The different packages of attitudes and practices that are associated with the term "liberalism" are of great concern to older, conservative Christians because historically, loose attitudes towards the authority of the scriptures have led to a watering down of convictions with the resulting loss of faith and declining influence.

Exhibit A for conservative disciples has often been the Disciples of Christ denomination, a fading mainstream religious organization that historically descended from the influence of Alexander Campbell's teaching in his later years. One hundred years ago, the Disciples were much more powerful in influence and numbers than their more conservative counterparts in known independent churches of Christ. However, the loss of conviction and compromise with worldly trends in religion, sociology and science have left the denomination a shell of its former self. This is the long-term result of liberalism and its spirit of compromise. Even among slightly more conservative independent Christian churches that have some thriving local groups, entertainment-oriented worship styles are making strong inroads and their teaching sometimes sounds like traditional Protestantism as they invite the lost to "receive Jesus Christ into their hearts as personal Savior."[55]

Concerns about the leavening influence of liberalism with its tendency to de-emphasize a strict construction approach to the Bible make lessons on Bible authority a strong priority with disciples who believe in a rational approach to Bible study. However, lessons that emphasize the importance of having "book, chapter and verse" to authorize our practices sometimes seem to stir little enthusiasm among younger disciples affected by Postmodernism. "What about the fact that different people interpret the Bible in different ways?" they ask, forgetting that there are disastrously wrong interpretations out there!

Institutionalism

Institutionalism was the big issue among known churches of Christ in the 1950's and in some places in the early 1960's. Institutionalism is seeing God's church as a network of congregations rather than saved individuals. The growing influence of that concept in the 1950's led to the insistence that loyal congregations of the network support parachurch organizations like orphans homes, clinics and Bible colleges and schools. Though for many, the primary problem was whether there was Bible authority for churches to send contributions to the brotherhood institutions, the even more fundamental issue was whether God's church was a network of congregations that could collectively sponsor such institutions or whether it is simply saved individuals that by definition can't have such adjuncts.

Christians in my parents' generation suffered greatly in the 1950's and 1960's because of their opposition to institutionalism. Promoters of the institutions labeled them as "antis," quarantined them and belittled them. To be fair, some opponents of institutionalism were just as acrimonious and personal in defending their position as the promoters, but the latter had the numbers, the money and the support of most influential leaders at their disposition.

My father lost meetings, preaching opportunities and friends because of his opposition to congregational support of brotherhood orphans homes, colleges, radio programs and other projects. Others were fired, mocked and ridiculed simply because they couldn't conscientiously go along with the denominational machinery.

Fast forward fifty years and many young disciples have no memory of the battles over institutionalism and know few people if any who suffered through them. It is difficult for them to see institutional concepts as a big enemy, because as in the case of Evangelicals, they seem so insignificant when compared to the evils of our godless world. This indifference concerns many older disciples, who in their lifetimes have seen great departures from the simplicity taught by Jesus as mainstream churches have solidified their status as the "Church of Christ denomination." In Latin America and other parts of the world, those taught by mainstream missionaries have taken institutional concepts to their logical conclusions and formed national "Church of Christ" organizations complete with national officers: presidents, vice-presidents, etc. In some cases the organizations have used their legal status to try to bully independent disciples into submission. However, most young disciples in this country have never seen such excesses and therefore have difficulty seeing institutionalism as a big enemy.

Not "Either or" but "Both and..."

What are the greatest spiritual enemies facing God's people today? Probably worldliness and lack of love! However, when look-

> *"What are the greatest spiritual enemies facing God's people today? Probably worldliness and lack of love!"*

ing at the greatest perceived enemies of many older disciples (false doctrines, liberalism, institutionalism, etc.) versus those of younger Christians (traditionalism, lack of emphasis on grace, etc.), which is greater? Of course, the truth is that all of the above are dangers to God's people. Perhaps the greatest danger is to focus on only one set of dangers!

I remember expressing concern to a godly young Christian woman about a congregation that was allowing elements of entertainment-oriented worship into their services. She sympathized a bit but then asked, "Which does God hate worse, clapping in rhythm with the singing? Or, dragging through a routine service with little enthusiasm?"

Though I probably should have answered instantly, I hesitated a bit before responding correctly, "He would hate the routine worship given with little love." Isaiah, Amos, Malachi and other Old Testament prophets would back me up on that (chapters 1, 5 and 1 respectively). Her point was that though I wasn't wrong to be concerned about one danger that usually concerns older disciples, I should perhaps be even more concerned with the evil that usually turns off younger ones.

May God help us to focus on all evils that Satan uses to threaten us, not just those that are popular to complain about among our peers!

Questions for thought

1. What are some ways we have been blessed spiritually by those of mainstream religious denominations and others with whom we've disagreed?

2. Why is it important to be able to read books and watch videos produced by those with whom we disagree, and be able to distinguish between the good and bad in those books/videos? What are some Bible texts or concepts which back up that principle?

3. If someone is too immature spiritually to be able to distinguish between truth and error, should they be reading and listening to writers and teachers who mix truth and error? Do you know of examples of those who have been led astray by error because they were unable to distinguish between it and truth?

4. Why do religious movements that lose their convictions tend to shrink and eventually die?

5. Why do so many never see the inherent dangers of systems like institutionalism? Why is it important to educate ourselves about the consequences of unbiblical concepts like institutionalism?

Thoughts for prayer: *Thankfulness for the valuable Bible material, hymns and examples of courage that have come to us from people with whom we've disagreed; wisdom to distinguish between the good and the bad in the writings of such people; strength to avoid the debilitating loss of conviction.*

Chapter 10

Merging Conviction and Mercy in Dealing with Modern Challenges, Part 1

Т he following slightly abbreviated review of a mega-church's worship service in Australia saddened me, not only for the atheist that wrote it, but for the young people he described who thought that they were seeking God.

Shaken but not stirred by stadium-rock spirituality[56]

The promise of awesome worship. That's what got me rocking up to a Planetshakers meeting. And I wasn't disappointed. They said "awesome" 20 times. Planetshakers is a megachurch, which is like a spiritual mega-meal deal. Because we love you. And so does Jesus....

Standing outside Planetshakers surrounded by chirpy, bogan-cool teenagers fizzing with excitement, one of the two gay athe-ist friends I was with described the crowd as "very Australian Idol." Outside Planetshakers it felt as if we were about to see a rock concert. And we were. As the band fired up and went off like a frog in a sock, I thought: "I don't care what they're selling but I'm buying it."

Christian pop, '80s power anthems, Metallica meets Cheap Trick. A mosh pit for Jesus was jumping with teenagers in rapture and a balcony of Planetkids went off for Christ. Music blared from the stadium sound system while the screen seduced us with slick videos edited so fast the phrase "subliminal image" kept popping into my head. Lyrics flashed up: "Come like a flood and saturate me now." My favourite was "King of Glory, enter in."

The room was buzzing with anticipation. I felt like a kid expecting Santa to arrive. It felt as if Jesus was going to turn up any minute. Then out came the pastors. Middle-aged blokes peppering talk about Jesus with constant references to the footy, reality shows and McDonald's. Almost swearing with... plenty of "awesomes" thrown in to convince everyone they were down with the youth.

Then there were the plugs for the Mighty Men's night and Beautiful Women Seminar. Male volunteers were encouraged to get involved with the ladies' seminar.... Beautiful women. Mighty men.

Then the headline pastor came on, all charisma and awesomeness. He spoke of worship, sheepgate, building in salvation, sheepgate, sacrifice and a bloke called Eliashib. And more sheepgate. As people yelled, "Yeah!", "Amen!" and "Awesome!" I wanted to yell, "I don't get it". I love the way religion convinces people by making things deliberately incomprehensible and you feel too shy to say "I don't understand" lest you reveal your stupidity.

After "sheepgate" the pastor asked us to close our eyes and bow our heads. He urged people who had left Jesus, had never had him in their heart, or were confused, to raise their hands so they could be prayed for. He sounded like a real estate agent. "One over there, thank you, sir. Anyone else? I'll wait a few moments. Yes, one down the back." Dummy bidders anyone? Then bewildered-looking new disciples were led out by the old hands.

The crowd left believing they had been moved by God and touched by Jesus. They hadn't. They had been seduced by slick video packages and had their emotional desire for love, community and certainty met by manipulation. It wasn't the Holy Spirit; it was just people. Aren't we awesome enough? [57]

Entertainment-oriented Worship

Though most known churches of Christ could never reach the level of entertainment offered in the Australian mega church, it would be foolish to claim that elements of entertainment-oriented worship have had no effect among those influenced by the Restoration Movement. Drama teams, choirs, praise teams, applause, rhythmic clapping and other elements from the entertainment world have made their way into many gatherings for worship and more are on the way.

Compromise with Idolatry

God's frustration with the children of Israel for their idolatry is a theme throughout the Old Testament. However, the worship of idols among ancient Jews wasn't something that sprang up in one day. Before the actual idol worship there were several preliminary steps:

(1) Idols in the heart - The elders who came to consult with Ezekiel pretended to want to seek God, but had idols in their hearts (Ezekiel 14:2-4). God explained later to Ezekiel that their hearts were still greedy for unjust gain (33:31, 32).

(2) Desire to imitate idol worshippers - The children of Israel wanted a king to be like the nations around them (1 Samuel 8:20). That desire to be like the nations certainly must have influenced them to introduce elements of idol worship into their worship. It wasn't easy to be few in number with a vastly different religion in the midst of much larger and more influential nations!

(3) Mixing (syncretism) - Israelites gave their children names that included the term "Baal" which literally meant "owner" or "master." Even Jonathan and David had children with the term in their names, Merrib-baal and Beeliada (1 Chronicles 8:34; 14:7). Some think that these names were not meant to promote the idol, Baal, but rather refer to Jehovah as the "owner" or "master."[58] Still others suggest that 2 Samuel 5:16 and 1 Chronicles 3:8 indicate that Beeliada's name was changed to Eliada to avoid the bad connotation.[59]

As could be expected, the mixing of the worship of Baal and Jehovah can be seen even more prominently in the Northern Kingdom where Baal's influence was stronger. The Samaria ostraca are pieces of broken pottery from the time of Ahab that were found in Samaria. There is writing on the pottery that lists several dozen names of officials and taxpayers. For every two names compounded with the name of Yahweh, one was formed with Baal.[60]

(4) Worshipping Jehovah in settings usually reserved for idol worship - Solomon loved Jehovah at the beginning of his reign, but perhaps the beginning of his downfall was worshipping him in the high places, much like the idol worshippers did (1 Kings 3:2,3). Several good kings like Asa and Jehoshaphat removed some high places, but evidently not all (1 Kings 15:14; 22:43) and this made idol worship easier to reestablish in subsequent generations.

Second Chronicles 33:17 is an interesting verse. When king Manasseh repented in his later years, the people continued to sacrifice at the high places, "but only to the Lord their God." In this case, perhaps, the worship of Jehovah at the high places was a step in a better direction, but it indicated that the influence of idolatry was still strong, and this, perhaps contributed to the fact that the reforms weren't lasting.

(5) **Full-blown idol worship** - After the desire to imitate the nations and the mixing of the worship of God with elements of idol worship comes the full blown idol worship.

Compromise with Modern Idolatry

Certainly materialism and the obsession with entertainment are two of the biggest idols in our Western world of the 21st Century, distracting billons of minds away from the Creator and refocusing them on shallow, manmade objectives that provide no purpose for life.

It's with the entertainment world that many postmodern disciples are most tempted to compromise in their worship of Jehovah God. Anything that isn't instantly exciting, funny or amusing is boring, or as teens like to say it – booohrrring! The concept that learning from God's word and praising him reverently is fulfilling, edifying and satisfying doesn't seem to carry much weight with many. That requires the development of some depth and therefore doesn't satisfy the desire for instant gratification. Thus what is momentarily exciting or fun wins out over what is eternally fulfilling, edifying and satisfying. Therefore we see the "spiritual" laser shows, fog machines, mosh pits, rock concerts, choirs, bands, drums, electric guitars, standup comedy, etc., and yes it's all "awesome" and all "for Jesus."

As with Baal worship, the slide of disciples into entertainment idol worship isn't an overnight process but rather occurs by degrees.

(1) Idols in the heart - An elder confessed to a young Christian that he usually thought about football every morning when he woke up, before he thought of God! Of course, football isn't wrong in and of itself, but when it begins to take over the heart in that way, a dangerous step has been taken. The same thing is true about other types of entertainment. Some Christians seem so fascinated by movies, that the latest flicks

"An elder confessed... that he usually thought about football every morning when he woke up, before he thought of God!"

dominate their conversation. Others plaster the walls of their rooms with pictures of music groups or other pop celebrities. No, not all of these things are sinful in themselves, but if we're honest, we must acknowledge that so often they go beyond simple hobbies and pastimes and become idols in the heart, taking over our time and energy and distracting us from God.

(2) Desire to imitate idol worshippers - This seems to reveal itself first in the ways we dress.

I believe that the teaching I give that seems to have the least impact is on holy and modest clothing. When I tackle that topic (not one of my favorites), I often mention some types of clothing that are highly questionable to me and try to diplomatically ask that sisters reconsider wearing them—short skirts (sometimes with tight leggings underneath), tight pants and low-cut blouses. Sometimes at the following assembly several sisters wear the exact same outfits that I have just mentioned as being questionable. Though you might imagine that they are doing it to "be in my face" as if they were singing, "nyah, nyah, nyah, nyah, nyah," I don't think that most are being rebellious but rather just don't "get it."

I know that tight pants, for example, could not be comfortable. There are medical studies that show that they are unhealthy and can produce a syndrome called *Meralgia Paresthetica.*[61] However, the tremendous pressure that some feel to conform to the world's fashion dictates, an idol, makes the battle against tight pants an uphill one. I'm thrilled if some with whom I'm working go from super tight to only "a little tight." But I digress!

As we consider our service to God, sometimes we begin to envy the attention of those who have compromised most with the entertainment idol world, the "Planetshakers" who fill stadiums with thousands. Why are there so many of them and so few that seek God through his word? Certainly, we think, they must be doing something right and we must learn from them. We begin to imitate them.

(3) **More mixing** - As our desire to imitate popular but worldly trends grows, we begin to try to justify them as being "no big deal." We point out with some justification, that controversies about them have nothing to do with the weightier matters of justice, mercy and faith. Then we begin to allow elements of that entertainment world into our gatherings for worship, first something like clapping, then soon afterwards instrumental music. The instrumental music may start with something simple, like a guitar or piano, but it probably won't be long before there is a full-blown rock band.

(4) **Worship in the same settings as idol worship** - Concerts of "spiritual" music begin to take the place of regular worship. Spiritual celebrities begin to be featured in invitations to such gatherings. Little is said of Christ or his word, but rather about the talent of the artist or the fame of the preacher, whose messages often are little more than inspiring stories strung together with little meat from the word of God.

(5) **And finally, we often see a complete transformation to the idolatry of the world,** in this case, obsession with the entertainment world and celebrity culture with little regard for God. Someone once told me that almost all "Christian" rock groups, see their "Christian rock" as a vehicle to get into the mainstream music world. That is their primary objective.

Thought Questions

1. Why is entertainment-oriented worship ultimately unfulfilling? Why can unbelievers like the atheist who reviewed the "Planetshaker" meeting sometimes see this fact more easily than supposed believers?

2. What aspects of materialism and entertainment are blended into worship in our culture? What are some modern idols of this world besides materialism and the entertainment culture mentioned in this chapter? How are they sometimes incorporated into worship?

3. Think of Manasseh's worshiping Jehovah in the high places. Why does not completely leaving all the elements of idolatry when turning back towards God set the stage for future generations to return fully to idolatry?

4. Why must those who want to introduce worldly elements into worship be gradual to be successful? How can we protect ourselves?

5. Why do people in general and Christians specifically have such a strong tendency to want to imitate others?

Thoughts for prayer: For teenagers and others who are exposed to the most shallow and worldly elements of "Christianity" and then are tempted to judge Christ on that basis; for those sincere people caught up in worldly "Christianity;" for wisdom to recognize the introduction of worldly elements into worship and to oppose them with clarity and love.

Chapter 11

Merging Conviction and Mercy in Dealing with Modern Challenges, Part 2

Instrumental Music in Worship, A Brief Word

Three young Christians raised in rather conservative congregations went to a street festival one weekend. They were drawn to a small stage where a man was talking about Jesus and singing gospel songs as he played on a guitar. Several family groups, including a number of children were drawn to the stage. The production made a positive impact on many who walked by.

As they were returning home, two of the group began to talk about the use of the guitar in the presentation. Surely, they remarked, it wasn't sinful to use the guitar to sing praises to God, but rather it almost seemed to be a healthy accompaniment to the man's sincere and loving expressions of his love for Jesus.

In our world racked with violence, perversion and selfishness it is understandably difficult to see a kind man singing praises with a guitar accompaniment as an evil that threatens God's people and as a sign of compromise with idolatry.

And yet, if we want to imitate Christ and those early disciples who were taught by his apostles, we will not include instruments in our praise of God. It's a historical fact that early Christians did not use instruments of music in praising God in their assemblies and that such were opposed, sometimes vigorously for hundreds of years after Christ's death.[62] The fact that the term "acapella" (literally, "as in the chapel") means unaccompanied singing, shows that historically, praises to God were sung unaccompanied by instruments.

If our desire is to "restore" the simplicity taught to Christ's followers by his original disciples, we will choose to praise him simply with the fruit of our lips (Hebrews 13:15). If, however, we are influenced more by cultural trends and the desire to imitate the entertainment approach to worship that is becoming increasingly popular in the Evangelical world, opposition to instruments of music in worship will seem trite and even absurd. It all depends on our focus.

Certainly an emphasis on God's mercy should keep us from pronouncing final judgment on those who may disagree with us on this and of course other issues. We can even admire some things about people like the kind man who used his guitar in his efforts to reach out to others and talk to them about Jesus. However, the conviction that we need to limit ourselves to praising God in the way that he has requested of us will restrict us to the type of praise he has specially requested, the fruit of our lips.

Clapping in Worship

I was tremendously impressed with a group of young disciples in a Western state after spending a weekend with them. They obviously loved each other and were striving to show the love of God in their lives. The last night of our time together we gathered around to sing praises to God and I noticed that one of the leaders pulled out a large candle and lit it. That made me a little ill at ease, but someone mentioned that it was just to simulate a campfire, which seemed a little odd to me. Then, as we started singing, a few began clapping rhythmically with the beat of the song. I felt very uncomfortable standing at the periphery of the group as their clapping grew increasingly louder and their swaying to the music became increasingly more energetic. I was supposed to give a final exhortation after the singing and thought about using that time to challenge what was going on. However, I had never studied the issue deeply, and after consulting in whispers with a brother standing next to me whom I perceived correctly to also be concerned about what was going on, decided not to make a public challenge, but rather request a deeper study on a private level.

After we dismissed, I went to talk to the brother who had the most influence in the group and told him that I wanted to study the issue of clapping in worship with him by email. He lovingly accepted my invitation and we had a good exchange for a period of several months about the issue. I respected him highly then and still do, although unfortunately we came to different conclusions. The material I'm presenting on clapping in worship for the next few pages comes primarily from my exchanges with that brother. His response in essence was that opposition to clapping in worship stifles expression. I believe, however, that it helps maintain the simplicity and purity that God wants and keeps us from taking steps towards an entertainment-oriented approach to worship that in the long term gradually draws us away from him.

Is Clapping in Worship Wrong?

Is handclapping in worship presumptuous? Is it practiced because God wants it? Or rather, is it practiced for our own benefit, because we like it?

Handclapping among churches can generally be placed in two categories: (1) Clapping in appreciation (a) for brethren who are to be honored, (b) when a good point is made during preaching, and (c) at baptisms and (2) rhythmic clapping while singing hymns.

It is highly doubtful that handclapping found its way into congregations of the Lord because scriptures were analyzed and it was discovered that for centuries Christians were lacking in something that God had always wanted from them. It is more likely that it was adopted directly or indirectly from the "International Church of Christ," Pentecostalism or some other popular religious trendsetters. Later, scriptures were searched to justify a practice that had already begun.

Handclapping in the Bible

There are a few references to handclapping in the Old Testament. Some are quoted to defend the practice in churches today. Psalms 47:1,2 says, "O clap your hands, all peoples; shout to God with the voice of joy. For the Lord Most High is to be feared, a great King over all the earth." Psalms 98:8 reads, "Let the rivers clap their hands; let the hills be joyful together before the Lord." Isaiah 55:12 says, "And all the trees of the field shall clap their hands."

The last two texts are obviously symbolic and can be compared to expressions in Revelation of "harpers harping" (Rev. 14:2). Psalm 98 refers not only to clapping but to instrumental music in verses 5 and 6. Therefore, if the text authorized clapping in worship today, it would also authorize instrumental music.

Psalms 47 has nothing to do with rhythmic clapping to music. At most, it might be parallel to Psalm 150 which commands the use of instrumental music to praise God along with other fleshly, physical forms of worship of the Old Testament. It has no relevance in determining the kind of spiritual worship which God wants under the New Covenant.

There are no references to handclapping in the New Testament and absolutely no indication that it was a part of the worship of churches for hundreds of years after Christ. That fact should give pause to all who defend it in worship.

Handclapping to Show Appreciation

Clapping to show appreciation for others has been a part of Western culture for millennia. Since Christians are to honor each other (Romans 12:10; Romans 13:7; I Cor. 12:23,24), certainly applause could be one way we choose to show appreciation in appropriate circumstances. For that reason applause among Christians is common at birthdays, awards presentations at schools and other social events. The question is, should such applause be a part of assemblies whose designated purpose is to praise God?

To defend applause as a part of worshipping God, it has been pointed out that worship assemblies not only involve vertical communion with God but horizontal communion with brethren. As a part of that horizontal communion, it is reasoned, we can applaud each other.

It is absolutely true that worship assemblies involve horizontal communion, fellowship with brethren. Hebrew Christians were told to "consider one another in order to stir up love and good works" in the assembly (Hebrews 10:24,25). Ephesians 5:19 tells us to "speak to one another" in psalms, hymns and spiritual songs. Colossians 3:16 says that when we sing we are "teaching and admonishing one another." The latter two texts, however, give us the key to this mutual edification. It is not brought about by praising each other (although there might be occasions for encouraging each other with clapping), but rather by focusing together on "singing...to the Lord" (Col. 3:16), by making melody in our hearts "to the Lord" (Eph. 5:19). That expression, "to the Lord," is found all through the Old and New Testaments in reference to worship and indicates a point of focus. God's people in the Old and New Testaments have always had designated times to meet together to focus upon prayer and praise to the Lord. Though we greatly encourage each other in designated times of worship, it comes from a common effort to unite and sing and pray to the Lord, not to praise each other. In that designated time to give praise to the Lord, applause for each other becomes a distraction.

Some activities, such as eating meals together, are important for the growth of the body (Acts 2:46). However, they are completely out of place in the time that is dedicated for worship to the Lord (I Corinthians 11:22, 34). The same thing is true of applause for birthday celebrants, preachers, mothers, fathers, grandparents, etc. While appropriate and stimulating in some settings, it is out of place when we are together at a time that is designated for focusing on worship to the Lord.

Clapping to Show Approval During Preaching

Dave Miller quotes from the *Encyclopedia Britannica* in his book, *Piloting the Straits*, page 238.

When Christianity became fashionable the customs of the theater were transferred to the churches. Paul of Samosata encouraged the congregation to applaud his preaching by waving linen cloths. Applause of the rhetoric of popular preachers became an established custom destined to disappear under the influence of a more reverent spirit.

It should be obvious that applause has historically been associated with show business ("customs of the theater") rather than praising God. In our entertainment obsessed culture, it seems that Christians should want to disassociate themselves from that worldly current rather than move towards it.

Both the Old and New Testaments employ the same word, "Amen" to describe how God's followers express their approval of the message. It originally meant "firm" and came to mean "so it is, so be it" (Thayer, p. 32). While applause tends to focus attention on a performer or a speaker, saying "Amen" focuses on the truth of the message.

> *"It should be obvious that applause has historically been associated with show business... rather than praising God."*

Instead of expressing ourselves in a way not found in the New Testament, but associated more often with theater and show business, Christians should express themselves in the ancient, time proven method that all acknowledge to have God's approval. "Let all the people say, Amen!" (Psalms 106:48; I Cor. 14:16). We can say "amen" at the end of sermons and prayers and perhaps even discreetly while they are being presented if we're not distracting others by drawing attention to ourselves. This form of expression is found in scripture, focuses on the message, is associated with praise of God and is unquestionably right. The other is not found in the scriptures, tends to focus on the speaker, is associated with show business and is highly questionable.

Applause at Baptisms

One brother has stated sincerely to me,

> How often have baptisms been announced in churches, and such announcements have been met with silent smiles. Souls have been wrested from Satan's grasp– from the dominion of Satan to the dominion of God—saved for eternity. Yet, a church of 400 sits silent at such an announcement. Then they go home and raise the rafters with cheering and applause every time their football team scores! Unrestrained celebration when their football team is "saved," but quietness when newborn babes in Christ in their midst are announced. Isn't there something seriously wrong here?

Though there should be a distinction made between the hysteria of a football game and the spiritual joy of Christians, the brother does make a valid point—that brethren are usually too reserved when witnessing a spiritual triumph. And yet, is clapping the best way to express that joy? Should baptisms be accompanied by drum rolls, cheers, or other forms of celebration seen at ball games?

The fact that clapping at baptisms may not necessarily be considered worship, gives me pause in my objections to it. Perhaps it might be considered a matter of judgment. However, the danger that such applause could easily move into the worship services for the Lord make me prefer that announcements of baptisms be met with enthusiastic songs of praise unto the Lord, either directed or spontaneous, with hallelujahs and other expressions of praise.

Rhythmic Clapping to Hymns

Rhythmic clapping to the music of hymns is parallel in many ways to instrumental music as an accompaniment to singing.

Both offer something beyond "the fruit of the lips," the type of praise God has specifically requested (Hebrews 13:15). Both are unauthorized in the New Testament.

Several points are made in defense of rhythmic clapping to the music:

(1) Clapping does not have melody line or tone. It is thus not music and therefore does not take us beyond the type of praise specified by God, fruit of the lips.

(2) God wants us to praise him with our whole body.

(3) We can praise God as we kneel, stand, raise our hands and therefore it should be acceptable to praise him while clapping.

(4) Brethren have patted their feet and tapped their fingers to the rhythm of hymns for years without being questioned.

None of these points are valid as a defense of rhythmic clapping to hymns.

Drums lack melody line and tone and yet would be unauthorized in praise to God because they do not give God the "fruit of lips," the type of praise God has specifically requested in the New Testament (Hebrews 13:15). The question is not so much, is it music, which is often debatable, but rather, is it praise from the lips, the instrument specifically requested by God for praise in the New Testament?

God does request that we give our bodies as living sacrifices unto Him (Romans 12:1) and that we love Him with all our heart, soul and mind (Matt. 22:37) but such expressions of what we should give to serve him should not be confused with body parts used to express praise to him. If the concept of giving our bodies to the Lord authorized worshipping him with different body parts, then we would have to click our teeth, stomp our feet, snap our fingers, knock our knees together and make all kinds of strange noises in worship. Also, such would mean that those who were paralyzed in various parts of their body would be unable to worship acceptably. The truth of the matter is that the concept of worshipping God with all our being doesn't have to do with body parts, but rather with worshipping with all our soul, energy and love. And yet, the instrument of expression of that worship with all our being is specified, the lips (Hebrews 13:15).

It is an error to confuse the position of the body while praising God and the instrument used to give that praise. One, corporal position, is not specified; the other, the instrument is. A band director might tell a student, "I want you to learn to play the flute. I don't care if you play it standing up, sitting down, or even kneeling or lying down, I just want you to play it!" In such instructions, liberty is given as to the corporal position, but the instrument, the flute, is specified. God hasn't specified a body position in praising him in the New Testament. Therefore, we can praise him while standing, seated, kneeling, raising the arms, bowing the head, etc. Whatever corporal position one may take, however, he should use the instrument of praise which God has exclusively requested in the New Testament, the lips. The hands are not the lips!

A distinction should be made between the usually silent, incidental, isolated and unobtrusive patting of the foot sometimes seen while brethren sing, and loud, collective clapping. One doesn't justify the other.

Questions that Need to Be Answered

1. Does God specify fruit of the lips as the type of praise he wants in the New Testament age? (Hebrews 13:15)

2. If "fruit of the hands" (clapping) is an acceptable way of praising God in New Testament times then why not the "fruit of feet" (foot stomping), the fruit of fingers (finger snapping), etc. Why not the fruit of drums, the fruit of cymbals, etc.?

3. If God wants rhythmic clapping, did Christians generally worship him through the millennia in an unacceptable way if they didn't clap?

4. What is the origin of rhythmic clapping to music in the church? Is it from heaven or from men?

5. Is there any evidence of rhythmic clapping to music among Christians in the first century?

I want to be open to any thoughts or ideas from those who may think the reasoning here is wrong or inconsistent. But until these questions are answered, I feel it my duty to speak out against clapping in worship as a practice that will take us away from the Lord and the spiritual, "fruit of the lips," worship he has authorized.

It is true that there often needs to be more enthusiasm among brethren—more amens and songs or praise. But there doesn't need to be applause, rhythmic clapping or any other type of expression that would move us away from the simple pattern which God has given us.

Conclusion to the Chapter

Faithful disciples have always had to deal with issues that seem to flare up and later subside. I've only discussed two briefly, primarily because they deal with how we praise God collectively.

Some differences have to do with interpretations among those who see the scriptures in a similar way. For example, good brethren I know who see the scriptures as our pattern to help us imitate Christ and his early followers have differences over matters like Sunday night communion, the Christian's participation in military service, the nature of the indwelling of the Spirit, the application of 1 Corinthians 11:2-16, the rights of those who have been divorced unscripturally, the exact nature of Christ's emptying of himself when coming to earth, etc. Unfortunately, some of those controversies haven't been characterized by much emphasis on mercy and Satan has taken advantage of that fact.

Some differences, however, are caused by a desire to get away from imitation of Christ and, by extension, his early disciples, to become more like "the Planetshakers," or to follow other trendy currents of the Evangelical world. They have to do with emphasizing feelings over scripture, fun over edification and worldly wisdom over godly wisdom. By nature this type of difference is more faith threatening because it reflects a desire to imitate worldly trends and a changing attitude towards scripture. We should constantly ask God to give us wisdom to be wise as serpents and harmless as doves in dealing with them.

Thought questions:

1. Can we admire some people, such as the man singing at the street fair with a guitar, even as we realize that their approach is not ideal?

2. Why is it good to always ask, "Is this form of worship that I am contemplating really for God? Or, Is it for me?" How can we know if it is for God?

3. Discuss or think about the five questions about "clapping in worship" under that heading above.

4. Why are differences among brethren who believe in imitating early Christians usually less spiritually threatening than those that reflect an indifference towards the concept of having Bible authority and a desire to imitate trendy worship fads?

Thoughts for prayer: For mercy for kind people who express their love for God sincerely but not in accordance with God's ideals; for the wisdom to learn from their examples without justifying their errors; for strength to be satisfied with worshipping God as much as possible like the earliest disciples who were taught by the inspired apostles.

Chapter 12

The Need for Both Conviction and Mercy, Part 1, the Need for Conviction

Prosperous Christians tend to lose their convictions! That is especially true of Christians of the second, third and fourth generations. Of course there are exceptions to this rule, but it is generally true. First generation Christians are those who have left the world or religious error to follow Jesus. Second generation Christians would be their children, third generation Christians, their grandchildren, etc.

When making this point with some blogging friends who criticize seeking authority through Biblical precedents, one referenced Ed Harrell, a religious historian among known churches of Christ who has written extensively about the role of prosperity in changing attitudes among churches. He told me not to give too much weight to Harrell's points even though I hadn't referenced them. I pointed out to him that the fact that prosperity tends to lead to lessening conviction doesn't come originally from Ed Harrell (David Edwin Harrell Jr.) but from the scriptures.

The Cycle of the Judges

The cycle of Judges is summarized in Judges 2:10-19.

10 All that generation also were gathered to their fathers; and there arose another generation after them who did not know the Lord, nor yet the work which He had done for Israel.

11 Then the sons of Israel did evil in the sight of the Lord and served the Baals,

12 and they forsook the Lord, the God of their fathers, who had brought them out of the land of Egypt, and followed other gods from among the gods of the peoples who were around them, and bowed themselves down to them; thus they provoked the Lord to anger.

13 So they forsook the Lord and served Baal and the Ashtaroth.

14 The anger of the Lord burned against Israel, and He gave them into the hands of plunderers who plundered them; and He sold them into the hands of their enemies around them, so that they could no longer stand before their enemies.

15 Wherever they went, the hand of the Lord was against them for evil, as the Lord had spoken and as the Lord had sworn to them, so that they were severely distressed.

16 Then the Lord raised up judges who delivered them from the hands of those who plundered them.

17 Yet they did not listen to their judges, for they played the harlot after other gods and bowed themselves down to them. They turned aside quickly from the way in which their fathers had walked in obeying the commandments of the Lord; they did not do as their fathers.

18 When the Lord raised up judges for them, the Lord was with the judge and delivered them from the hand of their enemies all the days of the judge; for the Lord was moved to pity by their groaning because of those who oppressed and afflicted them.

19 But it came about when the judge died, that they would turn back and act more corruptly than their fathers, in following other gods to serve them and bow down to them; they did not abandon their practices or their stubborn ways.

1. Blessings and prosperity - The cycle starts with prosperity such as God gave the children of Israel after the conquest of Canaan.

2. Apostasy (verses 11-13) - Prosperous, blessed people tend to feel self-sufficient and begin to look at other gods around them.

3. Punishment, oppression (verses 14,15) - Departure from God's ways always lead to horrible results. In the case of the children of Israel the oppression came at the hands of nations around them that God raised up. In our case, it's often the terrible consequences that come from our sin.

4. Repentance, appeals to Jehovah - This point isn't clear in Judges 2, but in portions of Judges the people did cry out to the Lord when they were oppressed (3:9; 15; 6:7; 10:10-16). The latter text is especially interesting because God pointed out to them that their previous periods of repentance had not lasted very long. But it is a fact. Suffering people tend to cry out to God.

5. Deliverance, return to blessings (verses 16, 18) - God used the judges to deliver the Israelites and return them to point number one on the cycle. Soon afterwards, however, they would apostatize again (verses 17, 19) and the cycle would repeat itself.

Prosperity Followed by Apostasy
Throughout the History of God's People

The cycle is seen all through history of God's people and not only in Judges. When Jeshuran (Israel) got fat, he abandoned the God who made him (Deut. 32:15). That happened with Israel under Solomon and other kings of Judah and Israel. The prophet Amos condemned those at ease in Zion who lay on their ivory beds, lived in summer and winter houses and feasted on choice meats and fine wines (Amos 6:1-7). He certainly wouldn't have won any points with feminists by referring to the rich women of Israel as cows of Baashan (4:1).

In the New Testament Paul said plainly that those who want to be rich fall into temptation (1 Timothy 6:9). He didn't say that it was a sin to be rich, but that the desire for riches is accompanied by temptation. A big part of the problem of the church at Laodicea was at least the perception that they were rich (Rev. 3:17).

The Role of Prosperity
in the Development of the Traditional Roman Church

The first centuries after Christ saw Christians as a small and persecuted minority in the Roman empire. Though generally impoverished, they abounded in good works and love and therefore gained a number of converts from the increasingly decadent Roman culture. Though they had to battle heretics and had numerous exchanges among themselves about various doctrines, especially regarding the nature of Christ's deity, they were generally people of conviction.

However, as the years passed this began to change when Christianity became easier. Eusebius, the famous church historian wrote,

> On account of the abundant freedom [granted by the government] we fell into laxity and sloth. We envied and reviled each other, and were almost, as it were, taking up arms against one another, leaders against leaders with words like spears, and people forming parties against people.[63]

And thus prosperity and acceptance began to corrupt God's people, accelerating their transformation from a convicted and sacrificial family into convictionless masses that squabbled among themselves and eventually subjected themselves to a power hungry religious organization with a bloated bureaucracy.

"Pietism"

Gary Gilley dedicates an entire chapter in his outstanding book, *Is That You Lord?* to the effects of a movement called "Pietism" among mainstream Protestants. Though originally a healthy reaction "to the highly intellectualized orthodoxy that had become common in Lutheran and Reformed churches in the decades following the Reformation,"[64] it evolved into a "feelings first" system that lessened convictions. According to historians like Mark Noll, Pietism eventually paved the way for the theological liberalism of the nineteenth and twentieth centuries.[65]

William Nix summarized the loosening convictions that came from Pietism.

> Although Pietists adhered to the Inspiration of the Bible, they advocated individual feeling as being of primary importance.... The first generation of Pietists could recall and reflect on its grounding in Scripture while validly advocating the need for

individual experience. A second generation would stress the need for individual experience, but often without a proper Biblical... basis. This would leave a third generation that would question individual experience with no Biblical or doctrinal 'standard' to serve as an objective criterion....[66]

I mention Pietism here, not because it illustrates so much that apostasy accompanies prosperity, but rather because it illustrates what has happened when feelings begin to take precedence over scripture as authority.

Loosening Convictions in the Stone-Campbell Restoration Movement

Generally speaking (with some exceptions), the old pioneers in the early 1800s who accepted the call to leave human creeds and organizations to emphasize Christ's unpretentious teachings were simple frontiersmen with little worldly fame or possessions. They weren't ashamed to meet in brush arbors and ramshackle meeting houses.

Their children and grandchildren, however, began to enjoy the prosperity of the booming economy in the Midwestern United States, especially after the Civil War. With the increasing prosperity and with Christians of the second and third generation came the almost inevitable loss of conviction. The old country preachers, the humble meeting houses and unsophisticated ways of their parents and grandparents became sources of embarrassment for this up and coming group. An increasing number of preachers received their doctorates in theology from prominent universities. W.T. Moore and others promoted open membership with unbaptized members of mainstream Protestant denominations in Christian churches.

On December 1, 1889, R.C. Cave preached a sermon in the
Central Christian Church in Saint Louis that was full of
modernism, denying in part the inspiration of the Old Testament.[67] His sermon brought on a storm of protests, but within
a few years such teaching became common in "Disciples of
Christ" churches. Now, that organization is a shadow of its
former self, a monument to the loss of influence that always
accompanies loss of conviction.

The known brethren who opposed the denominational development of the Disciples of Christ and their compromises
with the world, for example their use of instrumental music,
were at first few in number and as far as their richer spiritual
relatives were concerned, insignificant. David Lipscomb is
often associated with that generally less prosperous group of
people, primarily in the Southern United States who resisted
the denominational tendencies.

However, the children and grandchildren of Lipscomb and
others like him, began to enjoy prosperity, especially after the
Second World War. Once again a denominational concept
about the church of Christ began to take hold and a loss of
conviction began to manifest itself among many influenced
by the Restoration Movement. They became concerned with
making "the Church of Christ" respectable with multi-mil-
lion dollar church buildings, nationwide radio and television
programs and other denominational machinery.

Now as we proceed in the twenty first century, many children
and grandchildren of those who opposed the development of
the "Church of Christ denomination" are themselves enjoying
prosperity and elevated social status. Thankfully, the tendency
to want to form and support denominational machinery isn't as
prevalent as it was in the middle part of the twentieth century,
but the desire to imitate entertainment-oriented worship and

discard a common sense approach to imitating Christ and his earlier followers is becoming more faddish.

For those promoting new approaches, it is always easy to find caricatures among traditionalists and then use them to trash the concept of seeking Biblical authority. Yes, there are black buggy Amish and gray buggy Amish that don't get along. The Troyer Amish split over hat brims. Some conservative brethren can be cranky, eccentric and divisive. Brethren I have known have split or almost split over the lettering on church signs, whether ties must be worn when serving the Lord's Supper, etc. Those who reject the concept of any pattern in the New Testament that would have a bearing on congregational worship and organization are quick to point out such mindless divisions. They say that such are the logical consequence of demanding Bible authority.

> *"It is always easy to find caricatures... The Troyer Amish split over hat brims. Some conservative brethren can be cranky, eccentric and divisive."*

However, as absurd as some divisions have been (and they come not from respecting the Bible too much, but rather giving too little emphasis to those scriptures that emphasize mercy), they are probably no more harmful than the jettisoning of convictions. If history teaches us anything, it is that loosening attitudes towards the authority of the scriptures eventually lead to apostasy and distancing of God's people from his will.

God isn't well served by convictionless denominations, entertainment-crazed megachurches or carefree groups of people who have taken the concept of authority out of the scriptures to the point that they don't know their purpose as congregations. Man doesn't function well without God's authority. The solution to the sometimes absurd divisiveness isn't a lessening of conviction, but rather a common sense application of the scriptures that emphasize mercy and longsuffering.

Questions for thought

1. Why do you think that increasing prosperity is often accompanied by a loosening of convictions?

2. In our prosperous culture, what specific things can disciples do to avoid the historical tendency to water down their convictions?

3. How many congregations do you know that have maintained their convictions and spiritual enthusiasm for over one hundred years? Name them. There aren't many! What has happened to most? What are some keys to using God's word to lay the foundation for long-term spiritual health for a congregation?

4. What signs have you seen that illustrate the fact that prosperity tends to lead to discomfort with plain, unsophisticated Bible teaching and a corresponding emphasis on respectability in the world?

5. Why doesn't man function well without God's authority? Why is the same true of churches?

Thoughts for prayer: The need for the ability to enjoy God's physical blessings without loosening convictions; the wisdom to provide teaching that will enhance a congregation's capability to maintain its convictions over a number of years; the humility to avoid being contaminated with the world's emphasis on money, sophistication and shows of social importance.

Chapter 13

The Need for Mercy

Emphasizing conviction without mercy and meekness results in the biting and devouring spirit that produces sectarian pride, fragments God's people and destroys congregations. Dee Bowman described the internecine warfare that characterizes disciples when they emphasize principles without forbearance. "We fight. We scrap. We war. We accuse. We assign motives. We designate sides. We recruit constituents. And we split. And split. And split. And then we split the splits."[68]

I like to read old copies of the *Gospel Advocate*, *Gospel Guardian* and other journals published in the nineteenth and twentieth centuries because they reflect the thinking of contemporaries of my great-grandparents, grandparents and others of previous generations. When reading them I find jewels of devotion and Biblical analysis. Unfortunately, however, I also find petty squabbling that reflects an ugly carnality. That spirit was more evident during times of controversy.

I remember reading a paper (I'm happy to have forgotten the title) where a writer constantly referred to his opponent as the "pope." As could be imagined, there was little if any serious biblical analysis in the article. It was almost 100% personal attack. I have heard debates where personal letters were read "to show just what type of person we're dealing with." In one such debate I attended, I knew that the person under attack was a godly person. And so, the debate quickly deteriorated into infantile name calling with few profitable references to the scriptures. Such a spirit has greatly harmed God's people.

• It violates texts like 2 Timothy 2:24-26 which commands us to correct with gentleness and James 3:13-18 which describes the wisdom from above as being the exact opposite of that exhibited in the controversies.

• It has greatly harmed the efforts of godly disciples to encourage a careful approach to Bible authority, because it has given the enemies of that approach a caricature that they can use for misrepresentation – "That's just the way all those legalists are!"

• It has discouraged thousands of young Christians who've said things to me like, "If that's Christianity, I want to have nothing to do with it."

• It treats the Bible as a kind of legal document that can be used to find fault with others or win personal battles with them.

However, the Bible is not a legal document to be analyzed as a prosecutor trying to find fault with others, nor as a lawyer trying to find loopholes; neither was it to be made into a list of do's and don'ts like the 613 precepts of orthodox Jews. It is not some vague narrative designed to give some kind of a hazy concept that we really ought to be nice to each other.

It is the story of God's people designed to teach us of God's unfathomable love and how to approach him. It gives examples to both imitate and avoid. Its warnings must be respected, but not turned into lethal weapons to attack others. It must be mined to extract its truths that give light and hope.

Judging

Perhaps the most abused phrase in the Bible is "Judge not and you shall not be judged" (Luke 6:37). Therefore, according to most people of the world, it is wrong to say that even the most heinous or perverted act is wrong. "That's judging!" they say piously and dare we say, "judgmentally."

Serious Bible students know that Jesus is referring only to the harsh, merciless judgment of the Pharisees and not to the righteous judgment (John 7:24) that he commands in numerous other texts: judgment to determine truth (1 Cor. 10:15, 16), judgment to help brethren work out problems (1 Cor. 6:1-6), judgment to warn of spiritual dangers (Phil. 3:18, 19, 1 Tim. 4:2, etc.) and judgment to discipline rebellious brethren (1 Cor. 5).

While some are quick to point out the types of judgment that Jesus was not condemning, they pay little attention to the fact that he was energetically condemning something—the ruthless, censuring spirit that is still seen today. Who do we think we are in pronouncing judgment as to who is going to hell? Even if we think that we have some scripture to back us up in making that judgment, the fact is that we do not know how far God's mercy will be extended regarding those who are incomplete in their growth or imperfect in their compliance. I might have been inclined to say that God would punish the Israelites for eating of the Passover presumptuously without cleansing themselves as God had commanded. However, God choose to extend his mercy to them (2 Chronicles 30:17-20). The same might be true of some today that I think might be punished by God.

Jude verse 9 is interesting for a number of reasons. There is much debate as to whether the reference to the dispute over the body of Moses comes from an ancient book, The Assumption of Moses, a Jewish tradition, Zachariah 3:2, a special revelation to Jude or another source. That, of course, has nothing to do with an application that needs to be made. It is probably sufficient to simply point out that Paul also made references to uninspired writers to illustrate points and such is probably the case here.

What is important is noticing the reserve that the archangel Michael had in confronting Satan. Though Satan's final destiny is obviously known, Michael did not feel it his place to "pronounce against him a railing judgment." He didn't want to tell Satan that he was going to hell, but wanted to leave that up to God!

If Michael the archangel showed reserve in pronouncing sentence against Satan, how much more careful should we be in avoiding "railing accusations" against our fellow humans. Frankly, such is blasphemy, taking for ourselves a right that belongs only to God. There is nothing "conservative" about doing that!

The careful, conservative approach when dealing with our friends who we feel lack growth and understanding is to mercifully correct them, "with a spirit of gentleness" (Galatians 6:1), even as we consider ourselves and our own spiritual challenges. We should pray for them as Hezekiah did for those of the Northern Tribes who did not cleanse themselves carefully enough (2 Chronicles 30:17-20). As we pray for them, we work to teach them more accurately the way of the Lord (Acts 18:26).

There is a line that must never be crossed by fleshly humans—that of pronouncing final judgment on a fellow human! We simply do not know how far God will extend his mercy. That is his prerogative! Yes, it is sometimes necessary to express our judgment that someone is in danger or even grave danger to try to shake them out of their spiritual stupor. But expressing concern for danger and pronouncing final sentence are two vastly different actions.

The same application needs to be made for the other extreme. Often when we highlight God's mercy, some take that emphasis as an indication that "everybody's OK," even when they ignore basic Bible principles. That approach is judging as well! It's judging that they are going to heaven even when they ignore or deny Bible fundamentals and that can be even more dangerous than presumptuously declaring that others are going to hell!

A woman in New York City felt a lump in her breast and went to her doctor to get it checked. The doctor belittled the woman's concerns and told her it was nothing and to go back home. However, the lump increased in size and finally after a year or so, she decided to go to another doctor to recheck it. The second doctor found that she had breast cancer that had already spread throughout her body. She passed away shortly afterwards.

Did the first doctor do the woman any favors by telling her she was fine, when she actually had breast cancer? Neither do we do anyone favors by acting as if everything were fine spiritually with them when they ignore basic Bible teaching. No, we do not need to "consign" them to hell, but we must seek ways to mercifully guide them to a better understanding of God's will.

A sensitive issue that lends itself to much misunderstanding is—how should we view our Evangelical friends? As much as we admire individual Evangelicals, the traditional Evangelical system has dangerous scriptural flaws that cannot be glossed over as if they represented no danger. For example, they teach that individuals are saved before dying to sin and being raised to walk in newness of life in baptism (Romans 6:3,4). It is a fact that in the first century no unbaptized people were considered Christians and most Evangelical scholars today would admit that. However, they teach that today there are unimmersed Christians. I've pressured some to give me a date or at least a century in which unbaptized people began to be considered true disciples and of course, they can't give me an answer. In essence they teach that some people are Christians today that Christ's inspired disciples of the first century would not have considered Christians.

Calvinism is an error that takes away the concept of personal responsibility and the need for repentance and therefore takes people away from God. The entertainment-oriented worship that is becoming increasingly popular among most Evangelicals represents a compromise with modern idolatry.

Though we may be able to share in some activities with our Evangelical friends, for example, opposing humanist projects in the schools, they must know that in spite of our great respect for many of them, we are gravely concerned about their errors and cannot conscientiously share with them in most of their projects. In most they will tell lost people to pray for salvation, raise their hands to accept Christ or give other unscriptural teaching.

Should we say that because of these and other errors we are certain that all who would categorize themselves as Evangelicals are going to be lost? Of course not! We would like to hope and pray that God will extend his mercy to many of them and even to others. But that is God's business. He will do the right thing. Whether those who have already died are going to heaven or hell is as one preacher put it, "none of our business." Our job is to demonstrate to those that are living and to others expressions of Christ's love, not glare at them across the room and be standoffish. Then we need to pray to God to help us to humbly show them more perfectly his way, even as we listen to exhortations they may have which may do the same for us.

Summary: Applying the Lessons of the Past in Imitating Jesus

An overview of the history of God's known people will teach two invaluable lessons to perceptive people of God:

(1) The loosening of convictions results in distancing from God. In the third, fourth and fifth centuries after Christ, the further his disciples went from the imitation of the early faithful disciples who were taught by inspired apostles, the less spiritual influence for good they had. This was true not only because they stopped imitating the spirit of sacrifice and service of the earliest faithful disciples, but also because they stopped imitating them in their simple worship and congregational organization. Frankly, those two aspects of imitation should go together. They are a package deal!

The loosening of convictions among the Disciples of Christ denomination in the last half of the 19th century brought on its waning influence.

(2) The neglect of mercy brings on a biting and devouring spirit that results in a weakening fragmentation of God's people. It needlessly divides congregations into warring camps that eventually die out as the children and grandchildren of the original combatants become disgusted with the whole setup and drift into the world or into feelings-first religious error.

In our corrupt world that so badly needs the gospel, we must accept the fact that God is not well served by the compromising spirit that gradually deadens spiritual fervor for heaven, while it mixes in a this-worldly focus that is dominated by social concerns. Neither is he well served by the suspicious and sectarian "shoot first and ask questions later" approach to religion that takes absolutely no account of his mercy.

In battling evil in our world, it is essential to have the spirit of Jesus. Those who are successful will be those who…

> …are not afraid to attack false religious systems (Matthew 23) even as they try to maintain a degree of friendship with some deceived by the systems (Jesus ate with Pharisee friends, Luke 7:36-50; 14:1-14).

> … are consumed by zeal (Jn. 2:17), and yet can be described as not bruising a broken reed (Matt. 12:20).

> … wise as serpents but harmless as doves (Matt. 10:16).

> … sharply rebuke those who are grave spiritual danger (Matt. 16:23), while giving time to those who are gradually sliding away from him (Rev. 2, 3).

No, Jesus wasn't contradictory in his approach, but rather was the perfect combination of conviction and mercy. We won't be successful followers of him unless we learn to become like him. Both errors: (1) conviction without mercy or (2) mercy without conviction will cause us to fall short. Constant meditation on Christ's life will help us attain that divine blend that will bless others here and eternally.

Questions for thought

1. Do you know of any churches that have fragmented because the members had no concept of God's mercy?

2. Have you seen some who treat the Bible as if they were prosecuting attorneys trying to find fault with others? Have you seen anyone treating the Bible as a lawyer trying to find loopholes? Why will such approaches take us away from Christ? What would be some more correct ways to describe how our approach should be to the scriptures?

3. Why is it important to learn to express concern for those in spiritual danger without pronouncing judgment on their destiny? What are some ways we can do the former while avoiding the latter?

4. Why do you think that some believe that being quick to condemn others is "conservative?" Why is such not the case?

5. What are some examples you can give of those who have done harm by judging that those with serious problems (whether medical, social, or spiritual in nature) are fine?

6. Why might some think that trying to mix conviction with mercy is contradictory? Why is that not so? What can you do in your life to successfully combine conviction and mercy to be more like Christ?

Thoughts for prayer: The desire to approach God's words not as prosecutors or lawyers, but as loving and obedient children seeking to know his will; wisdom to avoid the judgment that Christ condemns while applying the judgment he commands; forgiveness for the times we've misused the scriptures to defend our positions without letting them simply speak to us.

Notes for Chapter 1

1   A.T. Robertson, *Word Pictures*, http://www.studylight. org/com/rwp/view.cgi?book=col&chapter=002&verse=008 3/15/2012.

2   A.T. Robertson
3   Louis Hoffman, "The Three Major Philosphical Epochs" http://www.postmodernpsychology.com/Philosophical_Systems/ Overview.htm
4   Romans 6:1.

Notes for Chapter 2

5   "Rationalism," The Free Dictionary, <http://encyclopedia2. thefreedictionary.com/Rationalism> 3/19/2012
6   G. Richard Phillips, "Rationalism," *The Encyclopedia of the Stone-Campbell Movement*, Douglass A. Foster, Paul M. Blowers, Anthony L. Dunnavant, D. Newell Williams, Editors, Grand Rapids, Michigan, William B. Eerdman's Publishing Company, p. 625.
7   Valentine, Bobby, blog February 18, 2012. http://stoned-campbelldisciple.blogspot.com/2012/02/alexander-campbell-herme-neutier-of-word.html, April 4, 2012.
8   Doy Moyer, Post on Facebook, December 21, 2012.
9   Doy Moyer, Post on Facebook, December 24, 2012.
10   Stephen J. Gould, *Evolution as Fact and Theory Science and Creationism*, New York: Oxford University Press, 1984, p. 118.
11   The Skeptical Inquirer, http://atheism.about.com/library/ quotes/bl_q_SJGould.htm?.
12   http://recursed.blogspot.com/2009/09/irving-kristol-and-evolution.html, April 11, 2012.
13   D. Newell Williams, "Barton W. Stone" *The Encyclopedia*

of the Stone-Campbell Movement, p. 706
14   Williams
15   Everett Ferguson, *Church History, Vol. 1,* Grand Rapids Michigan, Zondervan, 2005, p. 193.
16   Ferguson, page 193.

Notes for Chapter 3

17   Richard T. Hughes, *Reviving the Ancient Faith,* Grand Rapids, Michigan, William B. Eerdmans Publishing Company, 1996, p. 183, 184.
18. 2 Samuel 11
19   http://californialetter.wordpress.com/2012/01/02/bibliolatry-churchianity-and-religiosity/, April 6, 2012.
20   Sewell Hall, "Let All the Earth Keep Silence," *Christianity Magazine,* Vol. 6, No. 10, p.5.
21   Colossians 3:16.
22   http://randalrauser.com/2011/01/keep-your-eye-on-those-so-called-christians-down-the-block/, November 23, 2012, quoted from Garrisoin Keillor, Lake Wobegon Days, p. 155-6.

Notes for Chapter 4

23   http://www.demographia.com/db-religlarge.htm, May 8, 2012
24   Francis Chan's comments on baptism could be found in April, 2012 at http://www.youtube.com/watch?v=wXuIvievIA0, Ap. (Or, simply put "Francis Chan baptism" into the Youtube finder and the video will pop up.)
25   John Milton, *Areopagitica*
26   Martin Halbert, http://userwww.service.emory.edu/~mhalber/Research/Paper/pci-lyotard.html, October 1, 2012

Notes for Chapter 5

27   Ashley Woodward, http://www.iep.utm.edu/lyotard/ October 1. 2012.

28   Jean-François Lyotard , http://www.marxists.org/reference/subject/philosophy/works/fr/lyotard.htm. October 1, 2012

29   Salman Ahmed Shaik, "Islamic Philosophy & the Challenge of Post Modernism" http://iba.academia.edu/SalmanAhmedShaikh/Papers/565992/Islamic_Philosophy_and_the_Challenge_of_Post_Modernism, October 1, 2012

30   http://www.npr.org/2012/03/26/149394987/when-god-talks-back-to-the-Evangelical-community, 8/16/2012.

31   Gilley, Gary, *Is That You Lord?* Webster, NY, Evangelical Press, 2007, p. 25-33.

32   Gilley, p. 29.

33   Gilley, p. 27.

34   Gilley, p. 31.

35   Gilley, p. 42.

36   http://en.wikipedia.org/wiki/Jean-François_Lyotard, October, 2012

37   http://www.zianet.com/maxey/patt4.htm, November 25, 2012.

Notes for Chapter 6

38   http://www.jewfaq.org/613.htm, October 1, 2012. Credit for the summation of the law in 613 precepts is usually given to Maimonides (1135-1204 A.D.) though it reflects the way Jews looked at the law for many years, even in the time of Christ.

39   E.P. Sanders, *The Historical Figure of Jesus*, London, England, the Penguin Press, 1993, p. 256.

40   Sanders, p.260.

41   Matthew 7:28, 29
42   Paul Earnhart, *Invitation to a Spiritual Revolution*, Studies in the Sermon on the Mount, Floyd's Knob, Indiana, Gary Fisher, 1998. p. 161, 162.
43   Alfred Edersheim, *The Life and Times of the Messiah*, Grand Rapids, Michigan, Wm. B. Eerdman's Publishing Company, 1974, Part one, p. 96.
44   1 Maccabees 1:15
45   "Philo," http://www.thefamouspeople.com/profiles/philo-256.php. September 21, 2012.

Notes for Chapter 7

46   "Sadducees," Robert E. Youngblood, General Editor, *Nelson's New Illustrasted Bible Dictionary* Nashville, Tennessee, Thomas Nelson Publishers, 1995, p. 1112.
47   D.A. Hagner, "Pharisees," *Zondervan Pictorial Encyclopedia of the Bible*, Merril C. Tenney, Editor, Grand Rapids Michigan, Zondervan Publishing Company, 1976, Vol. 4, p. 745.

Notes for Chapter 8

48   http://www.book-lover.com/bookworms/22606-8_26.html, November 28, 2012
49   J.D. Floyd "Recollections of Rees Jones" *Gospel Advocate*, February 6, 1911, p. 164
50   *Gospel Advocate*, August 16, 1900, quoted in J.D. Tant, Texas Preacher, by Yater Tant, p. 237.
51   Gardner Hall, *Foy Short, A Life in Southern Africa*, Port Murray, NJ, Mount Bethel Press, 2012, p. 52.
52   http://www.unity-in-diversity.org/Books/voc/page11.htm. November 27, 2012.

Notes for Chapter 9

53   Francis Chan, *The Forgotten God*, pages 23, 90.
54   Chan, page 55.
55   I like to listen to a preacher from Zarephath Christian church in New Jersey at 8:30AM on Sunday mornings. Though, I appreciate many of his thoughts, he is overly influenced by Postmodernism. I noticed last Sunday (October 29, 2012) that he invited his listeners to "receive Christ in their hearts as personal Savior."

Notes for Chapter 10

56   http://www.theage.com.au/opinion/shaken-but-not-stirred-by-stadiumrock-spirituality-20090728-e02k.html?page=-1, July 29, 2009,
57   http://www.theage.com.au/opinion/shaken-but-not-stirred-by-stadiumrock-spirituality-20090728-e02k.html?page=-1, July 29, 2009,
58   A.E. Cundall, "Baal," *Zondervan Pictorial Encyclopedia*, Grand Rapids, Michigan, Zondervan Publishing House, 1976, Vol. 1, p. 433.
59   *Zondervan Pictorial Encyclopedia*, Vol. 1, p. 505.
60   A.E. Cundall
61   http://us.gizmodo.com/5912709/skinny-jeans-are-damaging-your-health, November 15, 2012.

62   There are a number of quotations from early sources at http://www.bible.ca/H-music.htm. October 29, 2012.

Notes for Chapter 11

63   Eusebius, quoted by David W. Bercot, *Will the Real Heretics Please Stand Up*, Tyler, Texas, Scroll Publishing Company, 1999, p. 121.

Notes for Chapter 12

64   Gilley, Page 17.

65   Gilley, Page 20.

66   Gilley, Page 21.

67   Earl West, *The Search for the Ancient Order, Vol. 2.*, 1950, Indianapolis, Indiana, Religious Book Service, p. 260.

Notes for Chapter 13

68. Dee Bowman, *It's All About the People* (Harwell/Lewis Publishing Company, P.O. Box 3385 Lakeland, FL 33802, 2003) p. 143.

15636112R00083

Made in the USA
Middletown, DE
14 November 2014